Fruits of the Forest

COOKING WITH WILD FOOD

SUE STYLE

Photography by John Miller

PAVILION

For Erica, *sine qua non . . .*

First published in Great Britain in 1995 by
PAVILION BOOKS LIMITED
26 Upper Ground, London SE1 9PD
Text copyright © Sue Style 1995
Photography copyright © John Miller 1995

The moral right of the author has been asserted.
Designed by Janet James

The author and publishers believe the information
contained in this book to be correct and
accurate at the time of going to press. Cooking and
eating wrongly identified wild food can be fatal.
If ever in doubt, don't. Neither the author nor
the publishers can accept any legal responsibility
or liability for any errors, omissions or
mistaken identification of food that may be made.

A CIP catalogue record for this book
is available from the British Library.

ISBN 1 85793 3850

Printed and bound in Italy by New Interlitho

2 4 6 8 10 9 7 5 3 1

Typeset in Baskerville and Bodoni
by Dorchester Typesetting Group Ltd

This book may be ordered by post direct
from the publisher. Please contact the
Marketing Department. But try your bookshop first.

The publishers wish to thank the following copyright holders
for their permission to reproduce illustrations supplied:
Garden Picture Library: p.34, Wild Garlic by Brian Carter;
p.38, Woodruff by John Glover; p.57, Elderflower by Didier Willery;
p.67, Winter Savory by Clive Boursnell; p.67, Fennel by John Glover;
p.85, Blackberry by Neil Holmes; p.107, Hedgehog Fungus by Gary Rogers.
Natural History Photographic Agency: p.109, Slippery Jack by Martin Garwood.

Fruits of the Forest

Contents

INTRODUCTION

This is a book about good things to eat. All of them occur in various parts of the world, all have been tried and tested. The fact that they grow wild and are (usually) free for the picking is a bonus. You should be prudent in your picking, however. Find out about and respect any local laws on harvesting (in Switzerland and other places, for instance, mushroom picking is controlled as to timing and as to quantity). Choose your site: it is unwise to pick plants in areas which are clearly environmentally unfriendly, either because of the lead fumes of passing cars or the lifted legs of passing dogs. Mushrooms are a subject all to themselves, amply covered in the various mushroom chapters. Seek specialist help if you are in doubt – and perhaps even if you are not – and always listen to local advice. In many Continental countries a mushroom identification service is offered by trained professionals. As more people become interested in wild mushrooms, perhaps we may usefully follow their example.

Having located and identified your wild plant, pick it in prime condition and prepare it promptly. Remember, too, that though many plants contain valuable nutrients, prolonged cooking will destroy most of them. Some plants can be eaten raw; keep a light hand with the ones which do need cooking. Chanterelles, for instance, actually toughen with overcooking, quite apart from losing their stunning aroma and taste.

One of the nicest things about wild foods is that each has its own definite, usually quite short-lived season. In our supermarket-dominated existence they come to remind us of half-forgotten rhythms of life, of a pre-freezer age in which people knew how to appreciate what was fresh, seasonal and – above all – local. The first wild strawberries picked from a bank in early June, misty white elderflowers made into a refreshing syrup for hot summer days, and plump white field mushrooms glistening in the morning dew – all these are light years away from December strawberries imported from California, factory-bottled cordials and neat little button mushrooms grown on sterilised compost in darkened rooms. If we are lucky enough to have the opportunity, let us learn to know the wild foods of our neighbourhood, to use them and to value them aright.

Bettlach, Alsace, 1993-94

A NOTE ON RAW MATERIALS

Unless otherwise specified, oil is tasteless salad oil, vinegar is anything but malt vinegar, mustard is French, pepper is black, butter is unsalted, flour is plain white (US all-purpose) and sugar is caster (US granulated).

CREAMY DRESSING FOR SALADS

The following salad dressing is called for in several recipes in the book. Blend or process salt and pepper, 300ml/10fl oz oil, 100ml/3½fl oz vinegar, 1tsp mustard, 1tsp sugar or honey, 1 egg in a blender or food processor; thin down if necessary with a little cold water. Store in a covered jar or jug in the fridge for up to 4 days.

SPRING

DANDELION

TARAXACUM OFFICINALE

F: Pissenlit, Dent-de-lion. G: Löwenzahn. One of the more evocative sights of *la France profonde* in early spring is of be-bereted country people bending low in the fields, knife in one hand, basket in the other, gathering dandelions. Back home, delicious smells of bacon soon begin to waft out of the back door. Rough hands trim the tiny serrated green leaves, swirl them in copious cold water and heap them up in a salad bowl. Over the top, complete with sizzling fat, go the golden crusty cubes of bacon, into the pan goes a splash of home-made vinegar, a wooden spoon scrapes up all the crusty bits and the whole is dashed over the waiting salad. Supper is served.

The springtime gathering of wild greens is an old-established one throughout Europe. Emilie Carles opens her magnificent tale of life as a schoolteacher in her beloved Savoie (*Une Soupe aux Herbes Sauvages**) with a tantalising list of all the wild plants to be found growing beside the river, and which she would make into a soup: sorrel, plantain, nettles, lamb's lettuce, wild spinach, a sprig each of wild sage and chives – and, of course, dandelions. In the tiny village of Tschiertschen high above Chur in eastern Switzerland, eighty-two year-old Nina Vinzens sets off into the mountains as soon as the snows have melted to fetch a basketful of wild greens to make soups, tisanes and dumpling dishes. In Greece the springtime outing to pick *horta* from the hills, fields and rock crevices is still a regular Sunday feature. The fruits of these expeditions are used in salads and pies, large and small. A friend who spends some time each year on the Ligurian coast in Italy told me recently of her delight at being included in a sort of joyful spring ritual: the village outing to gather wild greens by the sackful, which are made into pasta parcels of varying shapes and sizes.

The dandelion has always been treasured for its therapeutic value. The plant's Latin name *Taraxacum* is apparently derived via the Arabic from a Greek word meaning 'disturbance' or 'disorder'; the medical use (= *officinale*) of dandelions for various disorders was recorded as far back as the tenth century by Arabian physicians. Over the centuries, all parts of this versatile plant have been used to sort out medical troubles as diverse as gout, rheumatism, warts, skin complaints and hyperactivity in children. The familiar and less elegant French name for dandelion evokes the plant's undoubted diuretic qualities.

Lest it be feared that dandelions are simply Good for You (the kiss of death for any food), it should be noted that they are also delicious to eat. They have been paid the compliment of being bred selectively to produce long tapering leaves and even greater roots. In some parts of Europe dandelions are earthed up or grown under pots like rhubarb in English kitchen gardens in Victorian times, to blanch and tenderise the leaves and make them less bitter. The roots are used by some to make a coffee substitute which (claims Richard Mabey in *Food for Free*) is 'almost indistinguishable from real coffee'. (Presumably when the book was first published in 1972, the British reader was unable to distinguish the difference.)

Wild dandelions are best harvested when the leaves are still dark green and not much longer than your little finger. When the tasty little infant buds begin to push themselves up from the heart of the plant, you can use them too. Soon the whole field is ablaze with yellow flowers (from which the dreaded dandelion wine, Miss Marple's favourite tipple, is made). Once the children begin to blow dandelion clocks, your time has run out and you will have to wait for next year to make your dandelion salad. As with many wild plants, the dandelion's leaves become coarse and bitter once the flowers have appeared. Wash the young leaves well and spin them dry in a salad spinner. They will keep for a day or two in the fridge in a plastic bag. Then use them in salads, soups, pasta dishes or pies. You can also blanch them or stir-fry them with other ingredients: their colour sets to a beautiful tender green and their aggressive nature is somewhat tamed.

Une soupe aux herbes sauvages, Émilie Carles, ed. Robert Laffont, Paris 1981

A Wild Herb Soup

Here is a spring pottage which takes its inspiration from Emilie Carles' book cited opposite. Use whatever is available to you, and serve the soup with a herb bread (page 73) or wild garlic bread (page 37).

SERVES 4

1 onion, finely chopped
1 tbsp oil
a small handful of each of the following, roughly chopped:
wild garlic; dandelion leaves;
lamb's lettuce, spinach; sorrel;
nettles
a few sprigs salad burnet, leaves only

1 litre / 1²/₃ pints (US 1 quart) chicken stock, or water + 2 chicken stock cubes
salt and pepper
2 large floury potatoes, peeled and diced
3 tbsp sour cream, or cream + 1 tbsp lemon juice
a small bunch of chives

Soften the onion in the oil without allowing it to brown. Add the chosen wild herbs, cover and let them wilt for 5 minutes. Moisten with the stock, season and bring to the boil. Add the potatoes. Cook for 15 minutes. Liquidize till smooth, return to the pan and taste the soup for seasoning. Whisk in the cream (or cream and lemon juice) and sprinkle the chopped chives on top.

Pasta in a Sorrel Sauce with Dandelions and Bacon

Dandelions often grow in the same pastures as sorrel. Pick them and put them together in this succulent spring dish of pasta in a pale green sauce topped with crispy bacon and wilted green leaves.

SERVES 2

FOR A LIGHT LUNCH OR SUPPER, OR COULD BE EKED OUT TO FEED 4 BEFORE A SUBSTANTIAL MAIN COURSE

150-200g / 5-7oz pasta
1 chicken stock cube
a handful young sorrel leaves, central ribs removed
150ml / 5 floz whipping or single cream (US light cream)
1 egg

salt and pepper
1 small onion or shallot, finely chopped
1 tbsp oil
100g / 3¹/₂oz bacon cubes
a handful young dandelion leaves
optional: a handful chives

Cook the pasta in boiling water with the stock cube according to the timing indicated on the packet.

Add the trimmed sorrel leaves to the pan of pasta for the last 2 minutes of cooking. Fish them out with a slotted spoon and put in the blender with the cream and the egg. Blend to a smooth purée. Season to taste. Drain the pasta and return it to the pan. Add the sauce and reheat very gently without allowing it to boil.

Soften the onion or shallot in the oil. Add the bacon cubes and fry them gently till just golden and crispy. Do not overcook or they will toughen. Toss the dandelion leaves into the pan and allow them to wilt slightly.

Serve the pasta in heated bowls with the dandelions and bacon scattered over the top.

WARM SALAD OF SCALLOPS WITH DANDELIONS, LAMB'S LETTUCE AND SESAME SEEDS

Not a dish for a dinner party because it requires you to be at the stove at the last minute, but worth doing for favoured friends for an informal supper in (or near) the kitchen: scallops are seared in olive oil and scattered over a salad of dandelions and lamb's lettuce.

SERVES 6

2 bunches dandelion leaves: about 100g/3½oz	1 tsp mustard
4 handfuls lamb's lettuce: about 100g/3½oz	1 tbsp plain yogurt
150ml/5floz oil	30 scallops with corals, dusted in seasoned flour
3½ tbsp vinegar	2 tbsp olive oil
salt and pepper	2 tbsp sesame seeds
a pinch sugar	4 tbsp balsamic or herb vinegar (page 70)

Trim, wash and spin dry the dandelions and lamb's lettuce. Make a dressing by liquidizing together the oil, vinegar, salt, pepper, sugar, mustard and yogurt to a smooth emulsion. Shortly before serving, toss the dandelions in some of the dressing and arrange them around the circumference of 4 large plates; dress the lamb's lettuce and heap some up in the middle of each plate. Pull away the band of muscle around the scallops and separate them from their corals. Toss both scallops and corals in the hot olive oil for 1-2 minutes – they should be just springy and lightly golden. Scatter them over the salads, along with the sesame seeds. Deglaze the pan with the balsamic or herb vinegar and drizzle this over the salads. Serve at once.

SALAD OF DANDELIONS, GOAT'S CHEESE, SOFT-BOILED EGGS AND WALNUTS

A lively spring salad, colourful and delicious. The dandelion leaves should be 5 or 6cm/2-2¼ inches long, when they are at their most succulent. Serve with any good bread or make your own herb bread (page 73).

SERVES 2

a good handful young dandelion leaves	a pinch sugar
salt and pepper	2 eggs, boiled 7 minutes, then cooled
1 tsp mustard	50g/scant 2oz fresh goat's cheese, cubed
300ml/10floz oil	
100ml/3½floz red wine vinegar	12 walnut halves

Wash the dandelion leaves well and spin dry in a salad spinner. Make a dressing with the salt, pepper, mustard, oil, vinegar and sugar. Toss the dandelion leaves in a bowl with some of the dressing. Then arrange them like the spokes of a wheel on two plates. Quarter the eggs and arrange them over the leaves. Scatter the goat's cheese cubes and walnut halves on top and drizzle on a little more dressing.

WARM SALAD OF SCALLOPS WITH DANDELIONS, LAMB'S LETTUCE AND SESAME SEEDS

MOREL

MORCHELLA ESCULENTA

F: Morille. G: (Spitz) Morchel. Morels only made it into this book by the skin of their teeth. The ground rules having been established that each wild food must have been personally picked and tasted, things were looking bleak for *Morchella esculenta* as the deadline approached. I read all that I could lay hands on about the growing habits of this most desirable mushroom. Morels are found from March to May (I read). They like the banks of streams (there is no shortage of water locally); freshly turned ground (we have lots of that, having just embarked on a new garden); bonfire sites (no problem, bonfires being a pleasure still permitted round here); grazing pastures (two a penny in deepest Alsace) and coniferous woods (the Black Forest is but a stone's throw away). Finally, they are supposed to do well on clay soils which – to the chagrin of my neighbours, who are more interested in champion carrots than roses – are typical of our area.

I combed the countryside, hunted beside the streams and meres of the Sundgau, checked the charred remains of any bonfire I chanced upon, scoured cowslip meadows, crept into dark and spooky pine woods. Not a morel in sight. I was about to abandon hope when I went to visit a friend over in Germany. Afterwards, as we said fond farewells on her garden path, my eyes strayed to her newly created flowerbed. Thrusting their way out through the recently applied mulch of bark chippings were two very succulent morels. I gave an excited yelp. In a magnificently generous gesture ('in

the interests of research'), she snatched them from beneath the roses and pressed them into my hand. After (ritual) protest, I bore them home, dried them and later shut them away with their marvellous aromas in a jam jar. I still haven't decided whether to use them or frame them.

Many people (myself included, until recently) have never met a morel in the flesh. A very distinctive mushroom both in aspect and in flavour, it is rather rare and enormously prized. The appearance and texture of the cap is a giveaway, pocked with pores like a tiny brown sponge or an irregular honeycomb. Some morels have a round top, like a tousled mop of hair; others are conical like a miniature Christmas tree. The colour of the cap can be anything from a light beige to a moleskin brown. The stem is always white. The entire mushroom, stalk and cap, is hollow, making it a good candidate for stuffing. Of the various types of *morchella* (all edible), the most important are the conical (*M. conica*), the common (*M. vulgaris*) and the round (*M. rotunda*). Good things come in small packages, they say; by the same token the smaller sorts (conical and common) are the most prized. If it is a large one, it will probably be a *rotunda*.

Because of their rarity, morels are always an excitement to find, and newsworthy. One of them sprang into our local paper recently, meriting a mention on the front page. Admittedly it was an unusually impressive specimen. Pictured athwart the folded newspaper

laid in front of its proud patron, it measured some 26 cm / 10½ inches in height (they normally stand 6 or 7 cm / 2½ or 3 inches high at most) and weighed in at 300 g / 10 oz instead of the usual 25-30 g / ¾-1 oz.

Fresh morels don't seem to me to have much of an aroma. It is in death that they give up their secrets. Best therefore, if you should be lucky enough to find some growing, to dry them. Spread them out in a dark, dry place on absorbent paper, or thread them like the beads of a necklace (not touching one another or they may go mouldy). Leave till dry, then shut them inside a jam jar or airtight tin. To use them, soak in cold water to cover until they soften (about 1 hour). Then lift them out with a slotted spoon (to leave behind the copious sand they tend to contain) and cut them in half. Soak again, in fresh water, for about half an hour. Then drain them and pat them dry. Once rehydrated, their weight will be tripled or even quadrupled. The soaking water can be used in any sauce you may be making, but filter it carefully through a fine cloth.

If you decide on a purchase of dried morels, check with your bank manager first. I recently strayed into a smart *charcuterie* on the main street of Arbois in the Jura, an area famed for its wild mushrooms. On the counter were three jars, like the old-fashioned sort used for boiled sweets, each containing a different variety of dried funghi: mixed mushrooms, ceps and morels. The price of each was displayed; in the case of the morels I recall only a lot of noughts, and it wasn't clear whether this was the amount per kilo or per hundred grams. I decided on the latter. Without a flicker, the suave *charcutier* carefully weighed and packaged a couple of handfuls of the little brown cones, punched keys on the cash register and asked if there would be anything else. No, that would be all. 'A hundred and ninety-six francs, please, Madame.' A quick mental calculation told me that I was about to invest some £23 in two handfuls of mushrooms. To say I had changed my mind (or my menu) would have looked unconvincing. The interests of research were once again invoked, the credit card produced and the test budget took a stunning blow from which it is still reeling. The purchased morels have now joined my own pair. Mine are bigger. And they were free.

PUFF PASTRY 'COFFINS' WITH SWEETBREADS AND MORELS

Years ago when on a trip to the Dordogne, we feasted on this wonderful dish at Le Centenaire at Les Eyzies. I asked the chef for the recipe, took it back to Mexico and taught it to my enthusiastic (Mexican) students of (French) cooking. It is wondrously rich; a light, probably meatless, main course should follow. The pastry and the filling can be prepared ahead, ready for assembly at the last minute.

SERVES 6

500 g / 1 lb 2 oz sweetbreads
salt
a slice lemon
50 g / scant 2 oz dried morels or
*   200 g / 7 oz fresh*
1 shallot, finely chopped
50 g / scant 2 oz (US 3½ tbsp]
*   butter*
250 ml / 8 fl oz dry white wine or
*   chicken stock*

2-3 sprigs wild thyme
250 ml / 8 fl oz double cream (US
*   heavy cream) or crème fraîche*
juice ½ lemon
a 500 g / 1 lb 2 oz piece best-
*   quality puff pastry*
1 egg yolk

Put the sweetbreads in a pan of salted water with the lemon slice. Bring to the boil, simmer for 2 minutes, drain and refresh. Chill the sweetbreads until firm.

If using dried morels, rehydrate them as directed on page 13. Wash fresh morels carefully. Drain and dry either sort on absorbent paper.

When the sweetbreads are firmed up, peel them and pull away as much membrane as possible, separating the flesh into little lobes; or chop them in smallish pieces. Soften the shallot gently in half the butter, then add the pieces of sweetbread, the wine or stock and the sprigs of thyme. Cover and cook gently for about 15 minutes.

Heat the remaining butter and throw in the morels. Cover and cook gently for 10 minutes. Strain the juices from the sweetbreads into the pan of morels. Put the sweetbreads aside and discard the thyme. Turn up the heat under the morels and give them a further 5 minutes' brisk cooking to reduce the liquid by half. Add the cream and boil hard again to reduce by half. Sharpen with some lemon juice and check the seasoning. Add the sweetbreads and bubble up together briefly. (Cool and refrigerate the filling if not to be used immediately.)

Roll out the puff pastry to a rectangle ½ cm / ¼ inch thick. Trim all the edges. Divide it into 6 rectangles. With the point of a sharp knife trace an inner rectangle on top of the pastries about 1 cm / ⅜ inch in from the edge, going not quite through the pastry. Mark cross-hatchings inside this inner rectangle, again going not quite through the pastry. Put the pastries on a baking sheet lined with non-stick paper and chill them.

About 20 minutes before serving, heat the oven to 220°C / 425°F / Gas 7. Brush the pastries with beaten egg yolk and bake them for 8-10 minutes or until well risen and golden brown. With a sharp knife lift away the inner rectangles (the lids) and scrape out any raw pastry inside. Return the 'coffins' to the turned off oven briefly to dry out.

Reheat the filling, spoon it into the 'coffins', put on the lids and garnish with thyme sprigs.

MOREL CUSTARDS WITH COURGETTES AND LEEKS

A delicate and delicious warm first course for a spring evening. The pale green custards are turned out and served over a lightly creamy sauce, with an optional garnish of fried quails' legs.

SERVES 6

150g / 5oz courgettes [US zucchini], diced small

100g / 3¹/₂oz leeks or spring onions (US scallions), finely sliced

salt and pepper

tarragon

3 eggs

300ml / 10floz double or whipping cream (US heavy cream)

300ml / 10floz chicken stock, or water + ¹/₂ chicken stock cube

25g / scant 1oz (US 1¹/₂tbsp) butter

2 shallots, finely chopped

20g / ²/₃oz dried morels, prepared as on page 13

4 tbsp dry white wine

optional: the legs from 3 quails sprigs chervil

Put the courgettes and leeks or spring onions in a small pan with half a glass of water, salt, pepper, and some finely chopped tarragon. Bring to the boil, cover and cook briskly for 4-5 minutes, then uncover and cook hard until the liquid is completely evaporated. The vegetables should be quite dry.

Tip them into the food processor or blender and allow them to cool a little. Add the eggs, half the cream and half the stock and process or blend till smooth.

In half the butter soften one of the shallots without browning. Add the morels and cook for 5 minutes. Add the wine and allow to reduce almost to nothing. Cool.

Lightly butter six 125ml / 4floz ramekins and put a disc of non-stick paper in the bottom of each. Divide the morels among the ramekins, then add the custard mixture. Put the ramekins in a roasting pan. (Cover with foil and refrigerate if not to be baked immediately.)

About 1 hour before serving, heat the oven to 180°C / 350°F / Gas 4. Remove the foil from the ramekins, add hot water to come two-thirds of the way up the sides and cover with foil again. Bake in the preheated oven for 30-40 minutes or until just firm. Remove them from the oven and allow to stand for 10 minutes.

Soften the remaining shallot gently in the rest of the butter. (Add the quails' legs to the pan now, if using them, and fry gently on both sides until just stiffened; remove.) Add the rest of the stock and cream and boil vigorously for 10 minutes to reduce somewhat. Check the seasoning. Reduce the heat (return the legs to the pan).

Turn out the custards, surround with the sauce (and quails' legs) and garnish with sprigs of chervil.

CHICKEN WITH SHERRY AND MORELS

One of the most famous dishes of the Jura (scene of my morel purchase) is *coq au vin jaune et aux morilles*, a classic combination of a humble barnyard fowl with two of the more expensive ingredients known to man: morels and *vin jaune*, a sherry-like wine aged for six years in small casks. Here is a slightly less ambitious (but no less delicious) rendering of the classic dish.

SERVES 4-6

1 free-range chicken: at least 1·5kg / 3¹/₄lb
salt and pepper
flour
25g / scant 1oz (US 1¹/₂tbsp) butter
1 tsp oil
1 shallot, finely chopped

20g / ²/₃oz dried morels, prepared as on page 13
a wine glass dry sherry
250ml / 8floz chicken stock, or water + ¹/₂ chicken stock cube
250ml / 8floz double cream (US heavy cream) or crème fraîche

Cut the chicken into 8 pieces and toss them in seasoned flour. Heat the butter and oil in a wide sauté pan or casserole with a lid. Fry the chicken on all sides until golden brown. Remove the chicken, reduce the heat and in the same fat fry the shallot gently without browning. Add the morels and cook gently for 5 minutes. Return the chicken to the pan and pour on the sherry, stock and cream. Bring to a simmer, then cover and cook gently for 25-30 minutes or until the chicken is just tender. Lift the chicken and morels out of the juices and keep them warm. Boil the juices down hard to reduce by half. Check the seasoning and adjust if necessary. Pour the sauce back over the chicken and serve.

PORK MEDALLIONS WITH MORELS AND MUSHROOMS

A quick and easy dish of tenderloins of pork with a creamy, mushroomy sauce. Risotto goes well as an accompaniment, or *Rösti* (page 132).

SERVES 4-6

25g / scant 1oz dried morels
2 pork tenderloins (about 750g / 1lb 11oz) cut in 2cm / ³/₄in slices
salt and pepper
1 tbsp oil
12g / scant ¹/₂oz butter

1 shallot, finely chopped
200g / 7oz mushrooms, sliced
juice ¹/₂ lemon
175ml / 6floz chicken stock
250ml / 8floz whipping cream (US heavy cream)
a pinch of dried tarragon

Soak, wash, drain and dry the morels as directed on page 13.

Season the pork slices, toss them in the hot oil and butter in a wide, shallow pan for 1 minute each side until light brown and crusted. Remove, keep them warm. In the same pan soften the shallot gently, add the mushrooms and lemon juice. Cover the pan and cook gently for 5 minutes, uncover, add the drained morels and cook 5 minutes more. Add the stock, simmer for 5 minutes, then add the cream and tarragon. Tip the reserved meat back into the pan and simmer for a few minutes more to reheat thoroughly and to allow the flavours to fuse. Check the seasoning. Serve at once.

NETTLE

URTICA DIOICA

F: Ortie. G: Brennessel. For some reason, nettle consumption seems to raise more eyebrows than almost any other wild indulgence. Yet the stinging nettle, though vicious, is extremely nutritious and its medicinal properties are also highly valued: the extracted juices have long been used as part of a spring clean-up plan, and the fresh or dried leaves made into a soothing tisane (*'pour les nerfs'*, explains my neighbour). Organic gardeners use nettles to make an effective fertiliser.

A rather smug old proverb recommends that fine maidens should 'drink nettles in March and eat mugwort in May, to stop so many from going to clay'. Some (balding) maidens use the leaves as a hair rinse, to arrest and reverse hair loss. Richard Mabey, in *Plants with a Purpose*, recalls that when cotton was scarce during World War One, nettle fibres were used to make military clothing. Even the sting seems to have its uses: like bee stings, nettle stings have always been considered helpful in the alleviation of rheumatic conditions and flogging with nettles (known as urtication) was practised for the relief (?) of pain by those unlucky Roman soldiers billeted in damp, cold Britain. A delightful little book lent to me by our local doctor talks of a *méthode héroïque mais radicale* ('a heroic but radical way') to cure gout by rubbing the

offending part with a bunch of freshly picked nettles. After that, mere culinary uses sound a bit tame.

Take the advice of W. T. Fernie in *Meals Medicinal* on the best time to pick them: 'If nettle tops are taken as a fresh young vegetable in the spring, and early summer, they make a very salutary, and succulent dish of greens, which is slightly laxative; but during autumn they are hurtful.' Pick them with rubber or gardening gloves, strip the leaves from the stalks, chop roughly and proceed to use them as in the following recipes. Contrary to what you might expect, nettles (once cooked) will sting neither your tongue nor your intestines: the toxic and stinging substance which lurks in the hairs beneath the leaves and on the stems is killed once it is heated above 85°C/185°F. In your anxiety to avoid potential urtication (to the stomach), do not overcook them: they contain considerable amounts of vitamin C and minerals which will be destroyed with prolonged cooking, and besides they will lose their excellent green colour. They don't taste peppery, just pleasantly fresh and grassy.

Because of most people's uneasiness about eating nettles, it may be best not to make a big production of the fact. Simply make up a dish, serve it and await the compliments. Then you can confess.

NETTLE AND POTATO SOUP

A rustic soup for springtime. It is important not to over-cook the nettles at the beginning so that they keep their fresh green colour.

SERVES 4

20 nettle tops, leaves stripped
   from stalks
1 onion, finely chopped
1 tbsp oil or bacon fat
1 litre / 1²/₃ pints (US 1 quart)
   ham or chicken stock, or water
   + 2 chicken stock cubes
2-4 floury potatoes,
   peeled and chopped
4 tbsp sour cream or
   Greek yogurt
chopped chives

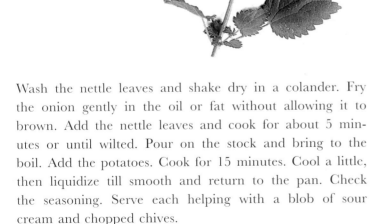

Wash the nettle leaves and shake dry in a colander. Fry the onion gently in the oil or fat without allowing it to brown. Add the nettle leaves and cook for about 5 minutes or until wilted. Pour on the stock and bring to the boil. Add the potatoes. Cook for 15 minutes. Cool a little, then liquidize till smooth and return to the pan. Check the seasoning. Serve each helping with a blob of sour cream and chopped chives.

FRESH HADDOCK FILLETS WITH NETTLE SAUCE

This fresh and delicate sauce goes well with fish, but be sure not to overcook it or it will go a dreary shade of khaki. Serve with rice.

SERVES 4

1 small onion, finely chopped
50 g / scant 2 oz (US 3¹/₂ tbsp)
   butter
20 nettle tops, trimmed, washed
   and chopped

300 ml / 10 fl oz chicken stock, or
   water + ¹/₂ chicken stock cube
600 g / 1¹/₄ lb fresh haddock fillet
seasoned flour
1 tbsp oil

Soften the onion gently in half the butter. Add the pre-pared nettle leaves to the pan, cover and cook until wilted – barely 5 minutes. Add the stock and simmer for 5 minutes. Cool a little, then liquidize till smooth. Return to the pan and check the seasoning. Off the heat, whisk in the remaining butter cut in small pieces. Cut the fish in 4 pieces, dust in seasoned flour and fry briefly in hot oil on both sides until opaque and firm. Pour the sauce on to 4 heated plates and put the fish on top.

PASTA PACKAGES WITH NETTLE AND COTTAGE CHEESE FILLING

Home-made pasta dough is rolled out fine, filled with a nettle and cottage cheese (or *fromage frais*) filling and served with Parmesan and olive oil. Serve a lamb's lettuce salad in addition for an original supper dish.

SERVES 4

**MAKES 40 PACKAGES EACH ABOUT
5 CM / 2 INCHES DIAMETER**

300g / 10oz strong white bread flour (US 2-2½ cups all-purpose flour)
1 tsp salt
3 eggs, lightly mixed
1 onion, finely chopped
25g / scant 1oz (US 1½tbsp) butter
40 young nettle tops, roughly chopped

1 level tbsp flour
100ml / 3½floz milk
100g / 3½oz cooked ham, diced small
150g / 5oz (US ⅔ cup) cottage cheese or fromage frais
2 chicken stock cubes
olive oil
grated Parmesan

To make pasta dough in the food processor, put the flour and salt in the machine. Switch on the motor and pour the eggs through the funnel with the motor running. To begin with, it will look a bit granular, then the dough should come together into a rough ball around the blade. If it remains grainy add a little oil. Turn out on to a floured board and knead vigorously (add more flour if necessary) until smooth and no longer excessively sticky – it should leave no trace on your hands. (If making dough by hand, put the flour and salt in a bowl, make a well in the centre and add the eggs. Work up to a smooth dough as above.)

Leave the dough to rest, covered with a damp cloth, for at least 1 hour.

Make the filling: soften the onion in the butter without browning. Add the roughly chopped nettle leaves and allow them to melt down a little. Sprinkle on the flour and cook for a couple of minutes. Add the milk and allow to boil for a minute or two, stirring. Remove from the heat. When cool, stir in the ham and cottage cheese or *fromage frais*. Chill the filling if not to be used immediately.

If using a pasta machine, cut the dough in 6 equal-sized pieces and roll it out thinly – up to setting No. 6 on a hand-cranked machine. Alternatively, cut the dough in half and roll out each half very thinly with a rolling pin to a rectangle at least 60 × 50cm / 24 × 20 inches on a large floured board or table. Put teaspoon-sized blobs of filling all over half the pasta sheets, brush with water around each mound, cover with the remaining sheets and press together well to seal. Stamp or cut out rounds or squares and place on a floured board or tray. Chill (or freeze) in one layer if not to be used immediately. (There will be quite a bit of waste – make ribbon noodles with leftover dough.)

Cook the packages for about 7 minutes in boiling water with the stock cubes until just tender – taste one to make sure. Drain, dribble some olive oil over them and serve a bowl of Parmesan to accompany.

NETTLE AND BACON QUICHE

Bacon seems to be a natural partner for nettles.

SERVES 3-4

AS A SIMPLE AND TASTY SUPPER DISH

100g / 3½oz bacon, diced small
100 g / 3½oz spring onions (US scallions), finely sliced
20 nettle tops, trimmed, washed and chopped
3 eggs
150ml / 5floz plain yogurt

150ml / 5floz whipping cream (US heavy cream) or crème fraîche
salt and pepper
200g / 7oz shortcrust pastry (US basic piecrust)

Fry the bacon gently in a saucepan until the fat runs. Add the spring onions and continue cooking until the bacon is a little crispy and lightly golden. Add the nettle tops, cover and cook for 5 minutes or until just wilted but still green. Whisk together the eggs, yogurt, cream, and salt and pepper to taste. Mix in the nettle and bacon mixture.

Heat the oven to 200°C / 400°F / Gas 6. Line a buttered 26cm / 10½ inch quiche tin with pastry and pour in the filling. Bake for 30-35 minutes or until risen and golden.

SALAD BURNET

SANGUISORBA MINOR OR POTERIUM SANGUISORBA

F: Pimprenelle. G: Pimpinelle. That salad burnet is beautiful to behold was recorded most poetically by Turner in his Herball of 1551: 'It has two little leaves like unto the wings of birdes, standing out as the bird setteth her wings out when she intendeth to flye. Ye Dutchmen call it *Hergotts berdlen*, that is "God's little birds", because of the colour that it hath in the topp.' Burnet was a favourite in medieval herb gardens, recommended as a decorative edging plant together with wild thyme and water mint so that when trodden on and crushed, they would 'perfume the air most delightfully' (Bacon). As its English name suggests, the leaves were also commonly used in salads. The Latin name is derived from *sanguis sorbere*, meaning 'to absorb blood', an allusion to the fact that it was used in poultices to staunch the flow of blood from a wound. Said to have been one of the

WILD SALAD BURNET

herbs exported by the Pilgrim Fathers to the New World, it quickly made itself at home in North America and reverted to the wild.

A perennial plant, salad burnet grows in meadows and on banks, its glossy evergreen fronded mounds making a bold statement all through the winter months and into early spring, when everything else is looking rather drab and dreary. Later on it forms attractive, raspberry-like seedheads tinged with red. You can pick it almost throughout the year, though it is in the early spring, when it is one of the few salad plants to have stayed the course through the winter months, that it comes into its own.

As with borage, its flavour is often compared to that of cucumber. Dr. Fernie in *Meals Medicinal* recommends its use, finely cut, 'so as to convey without any disagreement of digestion the desired flavour to those delicate persons who are debarred from the taking the real thing [i.e. cucumber]'. Its cucumber connotations are certainly pleasing and it makes a delicious mousse or soup. Strip the leaves from the stems (from top to bottom) and scatter them over fresh pasta (with an additional sprinkling of olive oil) or over potato salad. The plant's natural astringency is manageable if it is mixed with other salad greens (and especially whites, such as chicory – or Belgian endive in the US) and softened by a creamy, sweetish dressing. Or you can use it to flavour butter (as for wild garlic butter, page 35) and melt it gently over cooked vegetables to impart a subtle cucumber flavour. I particularly like to reserve it for decorative purposes: a couple of sprigs floating in a jug of Pimms or white wine cup look very fetching.

Spring Salad of Oranges, Chicory and Burnet

A salad of beautiful contrasts, best appreciated if served on a large white plate: a wheel of orange slices (alternating blood and navel) surrounds a pile of chicory dressed with a creamy vinaigrette. Little sprigs of burnet and snipped chives are scattered over the top.

FOR EACH PERSON YOU NEED

*1 blood orange and 1 navel
  orange, pared of peel with a
  sharp knife and sliced thinly
salt and pepper
¹/₂ head chicory (US Belgian
  endive), sliced very finely
1 quantity creamy dressing
  (page 6)*

*juice of 1 orange
8-10 sprigs salad burnet
a small bunch chives or spring
  onions (US scallions), snipped
  or chopped*

Arrange the orange slices in alternate colours, overlapping them slightly, around a large white plate. Season with salt and pepper. Heap up the chicory in the middle. Dilute the creamy dressing to a pouring consistency with the orange juice. Dribble some of it over the chicory slices (there will be more than you need for one person – refrigerate the rest for later use), so that it leaks into them and under the orange slices. (Do not pour it over the orange slices or they will disappear.) Leave for about an hour for the flavours to penetrate. Strip the leaves from the sprigs of salad burnet and scatter them over the salad, along with the chives or spring onions.

White Wine Cup with Salad Burnet Sprigs

When you want a refreshing and not-too-alcoholic white wine cup for a spring evening, try this one.

MAKES ABOUT 1·5 LITRES/2½ PINTS (US 1½ QUARTS)

*1 bottle fruity but dry white wine
1 orange and 1 lemon, sliced
optional: 1-2 tbsp sugar*

*several sprigs salad burnet
250 ml / 8 fl oz sparkling mineral
  water or soda water*

Pour the wine into a large glass jug. Add the remaining ingredients, stir well and allow to infuse for a few hours in the fridge. Add ice cubes just before serving.

CULTIVATED SALAD BURNET

MOUSSES OF SALAD BURNET AND FROMAGE FRAIS

Lightly set mousses (or make one large one in a soufflé dish) flavoured with salad burnet and served with strips of smoked salmon.

MAKES 8 x 125 ML/4 FL OZ RAMEKINS

slices peeled cucumber
salt
6 sheets gelatine or 4 tsp
  powdered unflavoured gelatine
250 ml / 8 fl oz chicken stock, or
  water + ½ chicken stock cube
a handful salad burnet sprigs
2 spring onions (US scallions),
  green part included

juice 1 lemon
pepper
250 g / 9 oz fromage frais or low-
  fat cream cheese
250 ml / 8 fl oz whipping cream
optional: 2 thin slices smoked
  salmon

Salt the cucumber slices and leave them to drain in a colander. Soak the sheet gelatine in a bowl of cold water until floppy, squeeze it out and add it to the stock. (Or sprinkle powdered gelatine on to the stock and leave till spongy.) Dissolve either sort in the stock by heating gently. Strip the salad burnet off the stalks, reserving some intact for the garnish. Chop the salad burnet and the spring onions finely in the food processor or by hand. Mix in the dissolved gelatine, lemon juice, salt, pepper and *fromage frais* or cream cheese. Liquidize until smooth. Whip the cream into soft peaks and fold it into the cooled mixture. Pat the cucumber slices dry with absorbent paper and place a layer in the bottom of each ramekin. Pour in the mousse and refrigerate till set.

Turn out and garnish with sprigs of salad burnet and strips of smoked salmon.

BEETROOT, LAMB'S LETTUCE AND NEW POTATO SALAD WITH SORREL DRESSING AND SALAD BURNET

For each person, take 2 or 3 large lettuce leaves and put them on a large plate, to serve as a base for the salad. In the middle put a heap of lamb's lettuce, and on top some cubes of cooked and peeled new potatoes. Around the heap of lamb's lettuce scatter some cubes of cooked and peeled beetroot. Make up the creamy dressing (page 6). Add a handful of sorrel leaves, trimmed and roughly chopped. Liquidize thoroughly until the dressing is smooth and pale green. Drizzle some dressing over the salad. Strip the leaves from a few sprigs of salad burnet and scatter them over the top.

BEETROOT, LAMB'S LETTUCE AND NEW POTATO
SALAD WITH SORREL DRESSING AND SALAD BURNET

SORREL

RUMEX ACETOSA

F: Oseille. G: Sauerampfer. Sorrel is one of those sharp springtime pleasures, like rhubarb, which the body somehow unconsciously craves as the days start to lengthen and the heavy diet of winter begins to pall. Richer even than lemons in vitamin C and full of iron, it is considered to be very good for you (unless you are unlucky enough to suffer from gout or are disposed to kidney stones, in which case it is to be avoided). Even the most robust person should avoid large quantities of sorrel because of its high oxalic acid content. However, the occasional spring time indulgence which is some people's lot cannot do any harm, could well do some good, and will certainly taste delicious. As Pepys's friend John Evelyn observed in the seventeenth century, 'sorrel sharpens the appetite, assuages heat, cools the liver and strengthens the heart; it is anti-scorbutic, resisting putrefaction; and in the making of sallets imparts a grateful quickness to the rest as supplying the want of oranges and lemons.'

This delicious herb, whose dark green, shield-shaped leaves look a little like spinach, can be found in grazing pastures and on roadsides throughout the year, but it is at its best in early spring when the leaves are tiny and new. As summer gets under way and the plant sends forth feathery sprays of pale green seeds edged with pink, the leaves become large and coarse and lose their freshness. If you live in a part of the world where the pastures in which they grow are topped twice for hay, you may get a second tender crop of leaves in the early autumn, coinciding nicely with the mushroom harvest – a happy coincidence, since sorrel and mushrooms seem to have plenty to say to one another (see page 99).

Beware recipes which suggest cooking sorrel in gallons of water for half an hour. By that time it will have dissolved into an unappetising khaki sludge and lost all its valuable nutritive properties. I like sorrel best either raw, used sparingly in salads, or blended raw into hot ingredients (soups or sauces) and then reheated to the barest suspicion of a boil. Thus its delicate fresh spring green is retained. It makes a good sharp contrast to rich foods like avocados, pork or oily fish.

When you have picked your sorrel and washed it well, bend the leaves together as if closing a book. Holding the leaves firmly together in one hand and the stalk in the other, yank the stalk upwards to strip it (and the central rib) away. If you wish, you can then cut the leaves across the grain into what the French poetically refer to as a *chiffonade* – ragged ribbons. Or proceed to use the sorrel as otherwise directed in the recipe.

26

SORREL ·GAZPACHO·

A stunning and simple chilled soup for a warm evening –
another recipe in which sorrel is used raw to conserve its
colour and fresh tartness. It is important to use a blender
(not a food processor), otherwise the soup will be simply
speckled, not smoothly green.

SERVES 4

*2-3 handfuls sorrel, trimmed and
cut in ribbons (page 26):
about 150g / 5oz
500ml / 16fl oz chicken stock, or
water + 1 chicken stock cube
4-5 slices stale white bread,
crusts removed, cubed: about
100g / 3½oz
250ml / 8fl oz single or
whipping cream (US heavy or*
*light cream) or crème fraîche
salt and pepper
optional garnishes:
cooked, peeled prawns (US
shrimp)
strips of smoked salmon
chopped hard-boiled egg
sprigs of chervil*

Put the trimmed sorrel leaves in the blender with the
stock and the bread cubes. Blend until quite smooth. Add
the cream and seasonings and blend again briefly. Chill
the soup well. Serve the chosen garnishes in small bowls
with the soup.

SMOKED SALMON QUICHE WITH SORREL AND CHIVES

A handful of smoked salmon trimmings, a few leaves of
sorrel, some snipped chives and the usual quiche ingredients make this a fresh and special lunchtime treat. Serve
with salad.

SERVES 2-4

*200g / 7oz shortcrust pastry (US
basic piecrust)
200ml / 7fl oz fromage frais or
plain yogurt
100ml / 3½fl oz whipping cream
(US heavy cream)
3 eggs*
*salt and pepper
a handful sorrel leaves, ribs
removed and cut in ribbons
some scraps of smoked salmon:
about 50g / scant 2oz
plenty of snipped chives*

Roll out the pastry and accommodate it in a lightly buttered 26cm/10½ inch quiche tin. Heat the oven to
200°C / 400°F / Gas 6. Liquidize the *fromage frais* or yogurt,
cream, eggs, seasonings and sorrel. Stir in the salmon and
chives. Pour into the quiche tin. Bake for 25-30 minutes
or until golden brown and set.

SORREL AND AVOCADO MOUSSES

A wonderful spring starter.

MAKES 12

6 sheets gelatine or 1 level tbsp
   powdered unflavoured gelatine
300 ml / 10 fl oz chicken stock, or
   water + 1 chicken stock cube
a handful young sorrel leaves;
   about 50 g / scant 2 oz,
   prepared as above
2 avocados
300 ml / 10 fl oz whipping cream
   (US heavy cream) or crème
   fraîche

200 g / 7 oz fromage frais or
   plain yogurt: natural or Greek
salt and pepper
optional extras:
10 quail's eggs, boiled 3
   minutes, refreshed in cold
   water and peeled
or 200 g / 7 oz smoked salmon
or smoked trout slices
some dressed seasonal salad
   leaves to garnish

If using sheet gelatine, soak the sheets in cold water until floppy. Squeeze them out and drop them into the hot chicken stock. If using powdered gelatine, sprinkle it on to the cold chicken stock, leave till spongy and then heat it until dissolved. Put the prepared sorrel in the food processor or blender. Pour on the hot stock/gelatine mixture, the avocado flesh, cream, *fromage frais* or yogurt, and salt and pepper to taste. Blend or process until smooth.

If using smoked salmon, line ten 125 ml / 4 fl oz ramekins with a slice each. Otherwise, oil the ramekins and divide the mousse mixture among them. (If using quail's eggs, bury one in each mousse.) Chill the mousses until firm – at least 6 hours or overnight.

To turn out, run a knife round them and give them a sharp tap on to a plate. Arrange some salad leaves around and top with a little extra fresh sorrel, snipped into ribbons or the pink tips of some flowering sorrel.

VEAL OR PORK POT ROAST
WITH SORREL SAUCE

A piece of veal or pork is browned in a casserole, then gently braised with spring onions and white wine. The sauce, made from combining the juices from the meat with the sorrel, is a poor colour but tastes delicious. Serve with fresh pasta or new potatoes.

SERVES 6

*a boneless piece of veal or pork:
    about 1·2 kg / 2 lb 10 oz, tied
    in a bolster
salt and pepper
1 tbsp oil
100 g / 3½ oz spring onions
    (US scallions), finely sliced*

*100 ml / 3½ fl oz dry white wine
a handful sorrel leaves, trimmed
    of central ribs
100 ml / 3½ fl oz cream*

Season the meat and brown it all over in hot oil in a casserole into which it will just fit. Remove the meat and lower the heat. Soften the onions gently, then replace the meat and add the wine. Cook in a moderate oven (150°C / 300°F / Gas 2) for 1 hour. Remove the meat and keep it warm. Tip the contents of the pan into the blender. Add the trimmed raw sorrel and cream and blend until smooth. Return the sauce to the casserole and bring to the boil. Reheat very briefly, then check the seasoning. Serve with the sliced meat.

SORREL AND AVOCADO MOUSSES

WATERCRESS

RORIPPA NASTURTIUM-AQUATICUM

F: Cresson des fontaines. G: Brunnenkresse. Most people are familiar with cultivated watercress, but fewer have the opportunity to see it growing in the wild. If you are used to the shop-bought variety, wild watercress (like most organically grown food) can seem unimpressive. The leaves are smaller and sometimes peppered with holes where the water snails and slugs have had a go; the plant is apt to be rather more straggly. Snip off a bunch of this fleshy green herb from its watery bed and rub a leaf between your fingers. Its pungent pepperiness will make your nose wrinkle up – the nasturtium part of its Latin name comes from two words meaning 'nose' and 'twist' – referring to the effect it is supposed to have on that particular organ. Its flavour, too, is deliciously peppery and its colour fresh and green.

In Britain in the last century, before fresh citrus fruits were available and accessible to all, watercress (which contains similarly high quantities of Vitamin C) played an important part in the diet of ordinary people. Richard Mabey in *Food for Free* quotes a charming passage from a nineteenth-century book describing hampers of watercress on sale in Farringdon Market in London. The watercress-seller would also do the rounds of the streets of residential areas, crying his wares. (Even Tennyson was a fan, lingering by his shingly bars, and loitering round his cresses.)

Besides its value as an anti-scorbutic, watercress seems to have been esteemed as a hangover cure. W. T. Fernie comments in *Meals Medicinal*: 'Persons who drink too freely overnight appreciate the watercress for its power of dissipating the fumes of the liquor next morning.'

Nowadays, sadly, it is best to be wary about gathering watercress from streams, mainly because it is difficult to be certain about the quality of the water in which it grows. Because it is rooted in the bed of the stream, you won't find it where there is a briskly moving current, rather a slowly meandering beck, and especially on its muddy edge where cattle come down to graze. For this reason, it can be a doubtful proposition for eating raw. Because of the dangers of disease (ranging from liver fluke to typhoid) from eating wild watercress, it is not always included in books on edible wild plants; if it is, its use is sensibly hedged about with if's and but's.

When I found some growing in a tiny stream down in the village, I consulted our local doctor, a great countryman and also a specialist in tropical medicine. (He seemed a little surprised that we would want to eat it – in our area, people are more interested in dandelions, lamb's lettuce and 'bear garlic'.) After consulting his medical books and questioning me on the stream and its environs, he recommended that we should not eat it raw. I think it's sound advice, and there are many delicious sauces and soups to be made with watercress.

If you do find it growing wild, listen to local counsel on the wisdom of using it. Cut it in early spring, before it becomes too large and straggly and certainly before it flowers. Don't wrench it from the stream bed, but cut off sprigs with a good sharp knife or scissors. If you uproot it, apart from destroying the watercress source for next year, you will get a lot of muddy, hairy roots, not to mention snails and perhaps even the odd crayfish – which seem to thrive in the same streams as watercress. Wash it thoroughly in vinegary water. Bring a large pan of water to the boil, drop in the leaves and boil for 5 minutes. Drain the leaves and refresh them with cold water to set the colour – an essential step if you want them to stay green. Then purée them and add them at the last moment to your soup or sauce. Or you can stir-fry them with other interesting ingredients. In this way watercress really comes into its own, rather than being relegated to the role of irrelevant garnish.

COLD CHICKEN WITH WATERCRESS DRESSING

A good dish for a spring lunch: cooked chicken coated with a cool green dressing of blanched watercress and *fromage frais*. Serve with new potatoes and a salad of lamb's lettuce with other seasonal greenery.

SERVES 4

1 medium-sized chicken, cooked and cut in 8 pieces, or 4 chicken thighs with drumsticks, cooked and cut in half
a large bunch watercress, leaves only: about 100g/3¹/₂oz, blanched, drained and
refreshed (page 31)
250ml/8floz fromage frais or Greek yogurt
salt and pepper
any jellied juices or 2-3 tbsp stock from the chicken

Remove the skin from the cooked chicken pieces and put them in one layer in a dish. Put the blanched watercress leaves in the blender or food processor with the *fromage frais* or yogurt, salt, pepper and any juices or stock from the chicken. Blend to a smooth purée and spoon it over the chicken pieces. Chill.

FISH PARCELS (OR CHICKEN BREASTS) WITH A COULIS OF WATERCRESS

Chunks of firm fish (salmon, turbot, halibut) are wrapped in brik (or phyllo) pastry, briefly roasted and served over a vibrant green watercress sauce. Serve with new potatoes, fresh pasta or rice. For a less elaborate dish, serve the same sauce with chicken breasts, fried in hot butter.

SERVES 8

8 fillets of firm fish; each about 150g/5oz, or 8 chicken breasts (US chicken breast halves)
salt and pepper
8 brik pastry leaves: 30cm/12 inches in diameter, or 8 sheets

phyllo: 30cm/12 inches square
200g/7oz trimmed watercress
100g/3¹/₂oz (US 7 tbsp) butter
olive oil

Season the fish (or chicken) lightly. Place the fish in the middle of a brik or phyllo leaf, fold the sides and ends up to make a neat parcel and place seam sides down on a baking sheet. Cover with a damp cloth and refrigerate if not to be baked at once. (Put the chicken breasts aside).

Make the sauce. Drop the watercress leaves in a pan of boiling water and cook for 5 minutes. Lift them out with a slotted spoon and put in the blender with a couple of tablespoons of cooking water. Purée with the butter, cut in small pieces, till smooth. Season to taste.

When ready to bake the fish, heat the oven to 220°C/425°F/Gas 7.

Brush the parcels with olive oil and bake for 7-8 minutes or until the fish (visible through the pastry) is just opaque and feels firm and springy to the touch, not soft and flabby. The parcels should be lightly golden and a little crispy. (Alternatively, fry the chicken breasts in hot butter on both sides until golden and just firm when pressed.)

Heat the sauce but don't let it boil or you will lose the colour. Check the seasoning, then pour a little on to each heated plate. Cut the parcels (or chicken breasts) in half and open them out over the sauce.

Prawns with Watercress and Spring Onion Sauce

Pretty, and tasty too: pink prawns on a green pool of watercress. Serve with rice or risotto. If you can get raw (grey) unshelled prawns, so much the better. Cook them on top of the onions and watercress stalks at the beginning of the recipe, shell and keep them warm while you finish the sauce.

SERVES 4

a large bunch watercress
2-3 spring onions (US scallions), chopped with green part
25 g / scant 1 oz (US 1½ tbsp) butter
40 large prawns (US medium or large shrimp)

200 ml / 7 fl oz dry white wine
salt and pepper
200 ml / 7 fl oz double cream (US heavy cream) or crème fraîche
some drops lemon juice

Separate the leaves and the stalks of the watercress. Blanch, drain and refresh the leaves as described on page 31. Reduce them to a purée in the blender, with a little of their cooking water to enable the blades to turn.

Soften the spring onions and the watercress stalks gently in butter. Add the prawns, white wine and salt and pepper. Cover and cook for 5-6 minutes. Lift out the prawns and keep them warm. (Shell if necessary.) Liquidize the cooking liquid and strain it through a sieve back into the pan. Add the cream, bring to the boil and reduce by half. Check the seasoning and sharpen with a few drops of lemon juice.

At the very last minute, stir the watercress purée into the sauce. Pour some sauce in the middle of each of 4 heated plates and arrange the prawns on top in a circle.

Smoked Pork Loin or Gammon with Watercress Cream Sauce

A joint of smoked pork or gammon is simmered gently, sliced and served with a sauce made from puréed watercress and cream. A *gratin* of potatoes goes well: finely sliced firm potatoes layered with the stock from the pork, dots of butter and a little finely chopped onion.

SERVES 6

1·2 kg / 2 lb 10 oz smoked pork loin or gammon
a bayleaf
1 tsp peppercorns
1 onion
1 clove garlic

a large bunch watercress, trimmed, blanched, drained and refreshed (page 31)
200 ml / 7 fl oz double cream (US heavy cream) or crème fraîche

Put the pork loin or gammon in a large pan, cover with water and add the bayleaf, peppercorns, onion, garlic and watercress stems. Bring to the boil and simmer for about 1 hour or until tender.

Put the blanched watercress in the blender with enough of the hot pork stock to enable the blades to turn. Blend until quite smooth. Add the cream and blend again. Lift the pork or gammon out of the cooking liquid and slice it fairly thickly. Lay the slices in an ovenproof dish and coat with the sauce. Refrigerate if not to be baked immediately.

Heat the oven to 180°C / 350°F / Gas 4. Bake the meat for 20-25 minutes, basting occasionally with the sauce, until hot through and bubbly around the edges.

WILD GARLIC

ALLIUM URSINUM

F: Ail des ours. G: Bärlauch. Bears, it seems, really do like wild garlic – hence the name of the plant in almost any language but English. Fortunately it's been a while since such beasts were to be found foraging in the forests around these parts. The only other company I meet as I cull my own wild garlic from among the wood anemones, oxslips and wild pulmonaria is the solitary woodsman and his chainsaw. He takes a welcome break from cutting up firewood for the annual spring wood auction, which takes place just as the 'bear garlic' comes into season. We exchange notes on the joys of *l'ail des ours*. He seems puzzled and a little wistful that these days few people in the village still come to pick it.

Our hens in Yorkshire in my childhood days seemed to share the bears' fondness for this pungent plant, though I recall that we were less taken with the end result – following their untimely escape into the nearby woods, the eggs they laid took on quite another character. They were just about acceptable for an *omelette à l'ail des ours*, but the four-and-a-half minute breakfast boiled egg was quite another matter.

I am, therefore, a late convert to this excellent wild plant. My uncle Gerald would turn in his grave if he knew. The woods behind his lovely old house set high above the river Tees in north Yorkshire were – to his great chagrin – redolent with it. Always distrustful of 'funny foreign food', he firmly believed that the garlic which infested his woods was the same as that he had met (and despised) in Mediterranean areas (he'd been in Palestine in the war, and alluded to it often). We – who had recently discovered 'real' garlic thanks to the books of Elizabeth David, and periodic sorties across the Channel – knew better. Or so we thought.

Years later I learnt that it is indeed of the same (*allium*) family and, if anything, even more delicious than bulb garlic. With wild garlic, instead of the bulb it is the leaves which are used. You get all of the wonderful garlic flavour, with the bonus of a stunning colour for your sauces and soups. Harvest it in early spring when it is still young, pale green and succulent. Stir a little into a risotto, or toss a few leaves into a salad of spring greenery. Combine some with spinach to make a delicious and original quiche; or wrap some leaves around a boned and skinned loin of lamb and bake in pastry.

WILD GARLIC BUTTER

Put a handful of wild garlic leaves in the food processor and chop them very finely. Add 150 g / 5 oz (US ½ cup + 2 tbsp) soft butter, salt to taste (if unsalted) and the juice of 1 lime (or ½ lemon). You should have a beautiful, bright green ointment. Remove it from the processor with a spatula and put it in a pile on a piece of foil or clingfilm. With wet hands form it into a rough bolster. Close up the foil or clingfilm and twist the ends like a Christmas cracker. Refrigerate for a few days, or freeze for a longer wait. A piece of it is delicious added to:

cooked pasta

cooked flageolets, French or broad (US fava) beans

roasted or grilled meats, especially lamb

WILD GARLIC NOODLES CARBONARA

A delicious lunch dish, to be served with salad.

SERVES 2

250 g / 9 oz wild garlic noodles   *200 g / 7 oz bacon, diced small*
(page 36)   *2 eggs*
salt and pepper

Cook the noodles in boiling salted water until *al dente*. Drain and put in a non-stick pan. Dry fry the bacon dice until the fat runs, then add them and their fat to the wild garlic noodles. Heat gently and crack in the eggs. Remove from the heat and stir until the egg is creamily set. Season. Serve at once.

WILD GARLIC SPÄTZLE

Spätzle are like little drops of dumpling made by extruding or slicing ribbons of batter into simmering water. Normally they are rather dull but these set to a beautiful green and are great with meat or game in a rich sauce, or with ham.

SERVES 6

a small handful wild garlic: *300 g / 10 oz strong white bread*
about 25 g / scant 1 oz   *flour (US 2-2½ cups all-*
150 g / 5 oz fromage frais   *purpose flour)*
3 eggs   *1 tsp salt*

In the food processor (or blender) blend together the wild garlic, *fromage frais* and eggs until quite smooth. Add the flour and salt and process everything to a smooth batter the consistency of a thick cake batter. Allow to rest for about 30 minutes before using.

Bring a large pan of salted water to a gentle boil. Tilt the bowl over the pan, allowing the mixture to come just to the lip of the bowl. Slice off ribbons of batter into the water by sweeping a sharp knife across the lip of the bowl. Repeat the process several times, then wait till some *Spätzle* float to the top of the pan. Remove them with a slotted spoon, refresh in cold water, shake dry and spread them out in a shallow dish. Continue with the rest of the batter until all is used up. Toss them in hot butter or oil just before serving. Or put them in a shallow layer in a lightly buttered ovenproof dish, dot with butter or *fromage frais* and bake in the oven at 180°C / 350°F / Gas 4 until thoroughly hot.

WILD GARLIC PASTA WITH 'LAMBURGERS'

This looks like spinach pasta but tastes more interesting. The 'burgers' are made from minced shoulder of lamb.

MAKES ABOUT 500G/1LB 2OZ NOODLES, ENOUGH FOR 4-6 PEOPLE AS A VEGETABLE ACCOMPANIMENT

800g/1¾lb boneless, trimmed lamb shoulder
salt and pepper
a handful young wild garlic leaves, roughly chopped
300g/10oz strong white bread flour (US 2-2½ cups all-purpose flour)
3 eggs
olive oil

Cut the lamb in cubes. Process to hamburger consistency in the food processor with salt and pepper. With wet hands, shape the mixture into 'burgers', each weighing 100-150g/3½-5oz. Chill.

Put the wild garlic leaves in the food processor with the flour and 2 tsp salt. Process till the leaves are finely chopped and the whole thoroughly mixed. Add 2 of the eggs and process till the mixture is in fine crumbs. Mix the third egg in a cup with a fork and (with the motor of the processor running) add only enough of it to have the mixture come together into a dough. Switch off. Turn the dough out of the processor on to a large floured board or working surface and knead until supple and no longer excessively sticky to the hands – add more flour if necessary to achieve this effect. Leave to rest, covered with a floured cloth, for at least 30 minutes.

On a huge floured board, or directly on the work surface, roll out the ball of dough to a large rectangle at least 50 × 70 cm/20 × 28 inches. Dust the top well with more flour and fold it over on itself several times (roulade-fashion). Slice the roll into ribbon noodles – I like them rather narrow, about ½ cm/¼ inch wide. Dust again with flour, lift and separate them with your fingers and allow to drop back on to the working surface. Leave quite well separated for several hours (or overnight) until using. If a longer wait is envisaged, allow to dry out completely, then put them in an airtight box or tin where they will keep for up to a week. Frozen, they will keep longer.

Cook the noodles for anything between 5 and 7 minutes, depending on how thin you have made them. Taste them after 5 minutes. When nicely *al dente*, drain them and return them to the pan with 1 tbsp olive oil and plenty of back pepper.

Grill or barbecue the lamburgers to the desired degree. Serve over the noodles with any juices.

LAMB FILLETS WITH WILD GARLIC SAUCE

This outstanding sauce, spring green and creamily garlicky, goes well with all manner of meats (especially lamb) or fish.

SERVES 4

2 lamb neck fillets: each about
    300g/10oz
salt and pepper
a handful wild garlic leaves:
    about 80g/ scant 3oz
25g/ scant 1oz (US 1¹/₂tbsp)
    butter

250ml/ 8floz chicken stock, or
    water + ¹/₂ chicken stock cube
125ml/ 4floz whipping cream
    (US heavy cream)

Season the lamb fillets and set them aside. Soften the roughly chopped garlic leaves in butter, add the stock and cream and simmer for 15-20 minutes. Liquidize till quite smooth, then push through a sieve. Return to the pan and check the seasoning.

Roast or grill (US broil) the neck fillets until done to your liking – between 8 and 12 minutes, depending on whether you like them slightly pink or grey and lifeless. Serve with the sauce.

BROWN 'BEAR GARLIC' BREAD

A good bread with cheese or soup, it also makes marvellous toast and a mean sandwich.

MAKES 1 LOAF

a handful wild garlic leaves:
    about 50g/ scant 2oz
300g/10oz strong white bread
    flour (US 2-2¹/₂ cups all-
    purpose flour)
200g/7oz (US 1¹/₂ cups)
    coarsely ground wholewheat
    flour

1¹/₂tsp salt
20g/²/₃oz fresh yeast or 1 packet
    (7g/ ¹/₄oz) fast-action dried
    yeast (US 1 package rapid-rise
    dry yeast)
about 300ml/10floz hand-hot
    water
2 tbsp oil

Chop the wild garlic very finely by hand, or in the food processor with a handful of the flour. Mix it into the flours and add the salt. Crumble or sprinkle the yeast on top, add the water and oil and work up to a firm, supple dough with your hands or using the dough hook of the electric mixer. The dough will be rather soft, but should not stick to your hands after about 5 minutes' kneading. (Alternatively, it should clean itself off the sides of the mixing bowl after thorough kneading.) If not, add sprinkles of extra flour. Leave the dough to rise in the bowl covered with a cloth or plastic bag until doubled in bulk – about 2 hours at room temperature.

Lightly oil a 26cm/10¹/₂ inch long bread pan. Knock down the dough, flatten it, roll it into a bolster the length of the pan and snuggle it in seam side down. Leave to rise for a further 25-30 minutes until it reaches at least the top of the pan. Heat the oven to 220°C/425°F/Gas 7 and bake for 30-35 minutes or until golden. Tip it out and tap the base – it should sound hollow. Cool on a rack.

WOODRUFF

GALIUM ODORATUM

F: Aspérule odorante. G: Waldmeister. Perhaps it was not by chance that John Fowles, in his book *The French Lieutenant's Woman*, named his principal character Sarah Woodruff. She was beautiful, mysterious, seductive, elusive, difficult to fathom.

Woodruff is all of these things. And like John Fowles' heroine, it tends to excite rather mixed emotions in people. Some love it, remembering festive Maybowls from their youth, others hate it and find its scent cloying and heady; it is rare to find anyone who is indifferent to it. A small, apparently insignificant plant which grows in beech forests and flowers in early May, it is recognizable by its little white starry flowers, and the delicate, upstanding green Elizabethan ruff of its leaves. It was a favourite medieval herb for garlands and potpourri; Benedictine monks patented the idea of using the flowers to aromatise wine – an idea which lives on throughout central Europe in the guise of the traditional *Maibowle*, a punch flavoured with woodruff. In the eighteenth century, King Stanislas of Poland is said to have attributed his good health and considerable vigour to the fact that he drank a daily infusion of woodruff.

'This is a favourite little plant', remarks W. T. Fernie in his quaint way (*Meals Medicinal*), 'which grows commonly in our woods, and gardens, possessing a pleasant odour, which, like the good deeds of the worthiest persons, delights by its fragrance most after death.' Indeed, when you stoop to pick the plant fresh from the floor of the forest in May and pause to sniff at it experimentally, you may wonder what the fuss is all about. Put the flowers, leaves and stalks in a dark, dry place on a fine linen cloth and come back to them in a few days; then you will understand. Complex, vanilla-like, sweetish aromas mixed in with the smell of new-mown hay will develop as the plant dries.

This curious smell, which develops even more strongly when the plant is dried, is due to the presence of a substance called coumarin. Woodruff seems to have a calming, even soporific effect on people – a fact noted and appreciated by medieval herbalists, and later attributed to the presence of coumarin. Still later coumarin was discovered to have important anti-coagulant qualities. Nowadays it is synthesised and is an important component in some products used to treat heart disease.

Some books warn against taking excessive doses of the plant because of the depressant effect of the coumarin contained. Few people, however, will be tempted to binge on woodruff, and a little of what you fancy may even do you good. A glass or two of a traditional white wine cup with woodruff flowers certainly seems to induce most soothing and pleasant feelings. Perhaps this accounts for some of woodruff's familiar English names: Kiss-me-Quick and Ladies-in-the-Hay. The unique aroma of the flowers combines well with fresh red fruits and the contrast of starry white flowers on purplish red fruit is striking. Woodruff can also be infused and made into a most excellent ice cream. An old Alsace cookbook gives a succinct recipe for a woodruff liqueur: a large handful of woodruff picked in May is to be infused for a month in a litre of *eau de vie* with half a kilo of sugar, stirred from time to time, then filtered and sampled.

Instead of imbibing it, you could always infuse woodruff in your bath water to help combat insomnia, or use it to fill pillows or sachets to freshen up your linen cupboard, or in potpourris.

RED FRUIT SALAD WITH WOODRUFF

Just as the first red fruits start to arrive, woodruff is in full flower in the woods. For this beautiful dessert, several fruits are used (cherries, strawberries, raspberries, red currants) and bathed in a coulis of strawberries. If you choose to include cherries, try to beg or borrow a cherry stoner; it makes life a lot easier. Otherwise leave the stones in and warn your guests.

SERVES 6

a small handful woodruff in flower
3-4 tbsp sugar
3-4 tbsp water
300 g / 10 oz strawberries, hulled

about 1 kg / 2¹/₄ lb assorted red fruit, trimmed and / or stoned
some extra woodruff, flowers and leaves

Make an infusion of woodruff by dissolving the sugar in the water until clear, then adding the woodruff to the syrup. Remove from the heat and leave for several hours. Strain the syrup, pressing down to extract maximum flavour. Put the strawberries in the blender or food processor with the syrup and blend / process until smooth.

Prepare and wash the fruit and put it in a large bowl. Pour the strawberry coulis over the fruit and turn it to mix well. At the last minute scatter some woodruff flowers and leaves over the top.

Parfait Glacé with Woodruff

Parfaits are perfect for the cook, because unlike most home-made ices they never freeze rock hard and can be sliced straight from the freezer. Serve a few strawberries with each, and some little almond biscuits or hazelnut tuilles (page 104) to accompany it. A garnish of a small sprig of flowering woodruff gives a helpful and decorative clue to the main ingredient.

SERVES 6-8

100g / 3½oz (US ½ cup) sugar
100ml / 3½floz water
a small handful woodruff leaves
  and flowers
3 egg yolks

250ml / 8floz whipping cream
  (US heavy cream)
2 egg whites
a pinch salt

Dissolve the sugar in the water, then drop in the woodruff and simmer for 5 minutes. Leave to infuse for several hours or overnight. Strain it and press down firmly to extract all the juice. Reheat. In one bowl beat the egg yolks until creamy, then add the hot woodruff syrup and continue beating until pale, thick and mousse-like. In a second bowl whip the cream into soft peaks and fold it into the cooled egg yolk mixture. In a third bowl beat the egg whites to a soft snow, but not so much that they are hard and granular. Fold them into the cream base. Line a 25 × 10cm / 10 × 4 inch loaf pan, that is 6cm / 2½ inches deep, with clingfilm. Pour the mixture into it and freeze until firm. Turn out and slice for serving.

Woodruff Ice Bowl

This appealing idea can be adapted to accommodate all sorts of flowers, wild or cultivated, and is guaranteed to elicit gasps of surprise and wonder. Take two mixing or salad bowls (pyrex, perspex or metal), one of them with a top diameter of 26cm / 10½ inches and one with a top diameter of 19cm / 7½ inches. Pour about 3cm / 1¼ inches of water into the bottom of the larger one. Add lots of woodruff (or other wild flowers). Freeze until just firm. Put a good base of woodruff and wild flowers on the ice and set the smaller bowl on top, centred. There should be a gap between the two bowls of about 3cm / 1¼ inches all round. Put something heavy (a can of beans) inside the smaller bowl to weight it down and stop it moving about. Pour in some more water and add more flowers. Freeze again. Repeat the process until the entire space between the two bowls is filled with water and flowers. You must do this in several steps, freezing each time, otherwise the flowers will all float to the top.

To unmould the ice bowl, run hot water over the outside of the big bowl and remove it. Pour some into the smaller bowl and remove it too. You are left with a shell of ice in which the wild flowers are suspended. Re-freeze until needed. Fill it with fresh fruit salad, or scoops of ice cream (such as the one below), and scatter woodruff or other wild flowers over the top. The bowl can be re-frozen and used a couple of times before it gets a bit leaky and starts to look a little tired.

SUMMER

BILBERRY

F: Myrtille, airelle. G: Heidelbeere.

CRANBERRY

F: Airelle rouge. G: Preiselbeere.

VACCINIUM MYRTILLUS AND V. VITIS-IDAEA

Picking bilberries and cranberries is very bad for the back – but wonderful for the soul. The early-morning forest is alive with the buzzings of busy insects, the mossy forest floor sounds softly hollow to the tread, the air is thick with the smell of toasted pine trees. But the slope is steep, the bushes hug the ground, and the little tin can or small bowl selected for picking (best not to be over-optimistic) seem to take forever to fill. To begin with, you despair of ever managing to assemble enough berries even to scatter over a breakfast yogurt, far less to furnish a bilberry tart or a cranberry sauce. Gradually your eye gets acclimatized and the berries appear more plentiful. Patience, in the case of picking both bilberries and cranberries, is more than a virtue, it is an essential prerequisite.

Bilberries – also known in Britain as blaeberries,

BILBERRIES

whortleberries and huckleberries – are found growing at medium altitudes in sparsely planted coniferous forests where the sun's rays slant obliquely through the trees. Cranberries (also known as lingonberries and cowberries) are sometimes found growing alongside them, though cranberries can grow at even greater altitudes, as high up as 3000 metres.

Both plants are of the ericaceous family, sharing the same habitat and often rubbing shoulders with freshly-flowering mauve heathers. The low-growing shrubby little bushes perform a useful ecological function (as well as a gastronomic one) by preventing soil erosion in places where the hillsides might otherwise be bare of plant life. When you see where they grow, at moderately high altitudes, on steeply rising ground beneath the pine trees, embedded in moss and pine needles, you marvel that they – or anything – can thrive here.

The leaves of both plants are dark green, shiny and oval; the cranberry's leaves are a little more elongated and curiously spotted beneath. Tiny pink flowers like little bells are followed by the berries which ripen in mid- to late summer, depending both on the altitude and on the weather in a given year. Bilberries are dark blue with an attractive bloom, while cranberries start out life white and end up a shining cherry red. The fruit is rather sparsely scattered on the branches of the small stunted bushes. As autumn progresses, the leaves turn a brilliant reddish-orange, making them an attractive sight on a mountain hike in October or November.

Still another sort of wild cranberry (*Vaccinium oxycoccus*) grows in peat bogs and other natural wetlands but is becoming increasingly rare as such habitats are drained and plundered. Its fruits ripen in September and October. Like sloes and roseships, they are said to be more palatable after the first frosts.

As the name *vaccinium* suggests, both berries boast some impressive therapeutic qualities. In folk medicine bilberries are used in gargles and mouthwashes. In the old days the juice was considered effective against typhoid, and in some country areas bilberries are still recommended for an upset stomach. The native Vermonter W. T. Fernie produced an appealing theory that bilberry pie was likely to be especially beneficial to consumptive patients because 'together with the

CRANBERRIES

bilberries, some of the moorland air from whence they come seems to be also swallowed; and perhaps reminiscences arise of the sweet fresh breeze, and the short, pleasant grass of the bilberry hills . . .' I always come away from a day of bilberrying in the Vosges feeling that the world is altogether a better place.

An aid to harvesting bilberries used in many parts of France is a sort of shovel-like 'comb': (*un peigne*). It looks a bit like a dust pan, armed with a row of teeth-like nails sticking out at the front, its collecting base like a fine grille. The holder lunges at the bilberry plant and with a sharp upward movement strips the berries off the branches and into the grille-bottomed part of the 'dust pan'. In Alsace, however, because this picking aid has proved altogether too brutal, the combs are increasingly frowned upon (indeed forbidden by the forest rangers) because they tear not only the fruit but also the greater part of the leaves from the stalks, and sometimes even the whole bush from its mossy floor. Better to use your fingers, and leave the plant for those coming on behind, and for another year.

Though the bigger cultivated bilberries (or blueberries) and cranberries (of turkey fame) are easy enough to find in shops, the wild version of either is seldom found on sale – which makes them even more fun to pick, because of the challenge and the rarity. Wild bilberries are fairly perishable (unlike cultivated, imported ones, which seem to be bulletproof) and should be eaten raw rather promptly after picking, or made up into tarts, jams or jellies; wild cranberries, on the other hand, are made of sterner stuff, as befits a fruit which can be found at such inhospitable altitudes. They can be kept in a screwtop jar in the fridge for several months without coming to any harm, or deep frozen. If you are bothered by black teeth after eating bilberries, take a tip from an old neighbour and chew on a slice of lemon.

SMOKED DUCK SALAD WITH BERRIES AND BLUE CHEESE

For this delicious salad, strips of smoked duck are tossed over mixed salad leaves with bilberries or cranberries and cubed cheese, and the rendered, crispy skin is scattered over the top. If smoked duck is difficult to find, use another smoked meat (ham, chicken etc) and omit the rendering of the skin.

SERVES 4

assorted summer salad leaves
100 ml / 3½ fl oz oil
2 tbsp vinegar: e.g. raspberry
    (page 82)
salt and pepper
1 tsp mustard
1 tsp sugar
150 g / 5 oz thinly sliced smoked
    duck breast
100 g / 3½ oz blue cheese: Stilton,
    Bleu d'Auvergne, etc, cubed
4 tbsp bilberries or cranberries

Arrange the salad leaves on four plates. Make a dressing with the oil, vinegar, salt, pepper, mustard and sugar. Cut the skin away from the duck slices and set it aside. Cut the meat into fine strips and arrange them on the salads with the blue cheese and berries. Divide the dressing among the salads. Toss the diced skin in a frying pan over a strong heat until the fat is rendered and the skin crispy. Scatter over the salads.

QUAIL WITH CRANBERRY SAUCE

The birds are briefly roasted and served with a startling sauce of cranberries with shallots and stock, enriched with a little butter and jelly. Use the same sauce for game, if you prefer, or for duck; serve with a gratin of potatoes.

SERVES 4

4 quails	100g / 3½oz wild cranberries
salt and pepper	300ml / 10floz game or chicken
thyme	stock, or water + ½ chicken
olive oil	stock cube
1 shallot, finely chopped	1-2 tbsp cranberry or redcurrant
75g / 2½oz (US 5tbsp) butter	jelly

Season the four quails, put a sprig of thyme inside each one, brush with olive oil and roast in a 220°C / 425°F / Gas 7 oven for 15-20 minutes or until just cooked but still a little pink.

Soften the shallot gently in about one-third of the butter. Add the cranberries and another sprig of thyme, cover and cook for 5 minutes or until the cranberries start to melt down. Add the stock and simmer steadily for 15 minutes until well flavoured and somewhat reduced. Fish out the thyme sprig. (Liquidize the sauce if you want it especially smooth and glossy. Return it to the pan.) Add any cooking juices from the quails. You should have about a cupful; if not, boil down further to reduce. Off the heat, whisk in the remaining butter bit by bit and just enough jelly to take the sharp edge off the sauce. Check the seasoning and adjust if necessary.

BILBERRY TART WITH NUT PASTRY

Bilberry tart must be bursting with fruit to be worthy of the name, so don't skimp on the filling. The tart should not be baked much in advance, otherwise the juices will gently seep into the pastry and make it soggy, rather than crisply nutty: prepare the pastry ahead, roll it out and chill it, and have the cleaned bilberries ready too. Then put the two together and bake briefly in a hot oven. Serve at room temperature with ice cream or whipped cream.

SERVES 4-6

125g / 4½oz (US ¾ cup + 2 tbsp) flour	60g / 2oz (US 4tbsp) butter
a pinch salt	2-3 tbsp iced water
3 tbsp ground almonds or hazelnuts	500g / 1 lb 2oz bilberries
	icing sugar (US confectioners' sugar) in a shaker, to taste
2 tbsp sugar	

Make the nut pastry: mix together the flour, salt, nuts and sugar and rub in the butter until the mixture resembles fine crumbs. Make a well in the middle and add enough water to make the pastry come together. Wrap in foil and chill. Roll the pastry out to fit a 26cm / 10½ inch quiche tin with removable base and crimp the edges decoratively. Chill the pastry case.

About 1 hour before serving, arrange the bilberries in the pastry case. Heat the oven to 220°C / 425°F / Gas 7. Bake the tart for 25-30 minutes or until the juices begin to run and the pastry is lightly coloured. Remove from the oven, sprinkle with icing sugar and cool on a rack.

GRATIN (OR CRUMBLE) OF BILBERRIES, CRANBERRIES, APRICOTS AND CHERRIES

A chic little summer dessert, to be served warm with ice cream. The fruit can be prepared ahead in the gratin dishes and refrigerated, but the sabayon requires a few minutes' attention just before baking. If sneaking away from the table in the middle of the meal to make disruptive noises in the kitchen is not your style, better to cover the fruit with a crumble (50g / scant 2oz (US 3½tbsp) butter, 50g / scant 2oz (US ¼ cup) sugar, 100g / 3½oz (US ⅔ cup) flour). Bake in the same way.

SERVES 6

6 large, firm, ripe apricots
200g / 7oz bilberries, with some
   cranberries if available
120g / 4oz wild cherries
2 tbsp kirsch or framboise
4 egg yolks

50g / scant 2oz (US ¼ cup)
   sugar
grated zest of 1; juice of 2 limes
100ml / 3½floz whipped cream
   (US heavy cream)
6 small sprigs of mint

Cut the apricots in 8 pieces each and arrange them in small gratin dishes. Scatter the bilberries and cherries around and over the apricots. Sprinkle with the liqueur. (Top with the crumble, if using.) Cover with clingfilm and refrigerate.

In a heavy-based ban (or in a bowl placed over a pan of barely simmering water) heat and beat together the yolks, sugar, zest and juice until thick and creamy, about the consistency of hollandaise sauce. The beater should leave soft tracks. Remove from the heat and cool. Fold in the whipped cream. Chill the mixture.

About 20 minutes before serving the gratins, heat the grill (US broiler) to maximum. If using the sabayon option, spoon the egg yolk-cream mixture over the fruit, sprinkle with a little more sugar and grill for 4-5 minutes or until just golden – do not go away: the gratins can very easily catch and burn. (If crumble has been preferred for the topping, bake the gratins in a 200°C / 400°F / Gas 6 oven for 10-15 minutes or until the crumble topping is golden brown.) Garnish with mint sprigs.

CHEAT'S BILBERRY JAM

No need any more to buy Bonne Maman's *confiture aux myrtilles*: here is a super-speedy jam for absolute non-jam-makers. Because of its low sugar content and brief cooking, the jam is not a keeper so is best stored in the fridge and consumed quite promptly.

MAKES 3-4 SMALL JARS

500g / 1lb 2oz bilberries
300g / 10oz (US 1½ cups)
   quick-setting jam sugar with

added citric acid and pectin
juice 1 lemon

Put the bilberries in a pan, bring to the boil and cook until the juice starts to run. Add the sugar and stir until dissolved, then boil for 4-5 minutes. Remove from the heat, stir in the lemon juice and leave to cool for 5 minutes before potting into small jars.

CHANTERELLE

CANTHARELLUS CIBARIUS

F: Chanterelle, girolle. G: Eierschwamm, Pfifferling. I pity the poor chanterelle. Other edible wood mushrooms enjoy an excellent camouflage. The brown cap of the cep (*Boletus edulis*) is near indistinguishable from the autumn leaves in which it nestles; the horn of plenty (*Craterellus cornucopioides*) resembles nothing more than the odd bit of rotting twig; truffles sensibly stay below ground. But the chanterelle leaps up at you from the forest floor, its deep egg yolk colour a dead giveaway. It reminds me of the poor shrew mouse which stands up on its hind legs and pipes pathetically at my prowling cat.

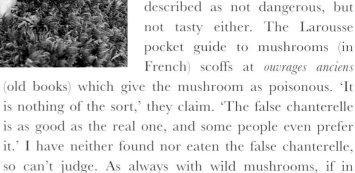

To make things worse, chanterelles often thoughtfully position themselves on a nice bed of bright green moss. Shafts of sunlight slanting through the trees pick them out mercilessly. Besides, they seldom stand alone, but group themselves conveniently (for the mushroomer) around the foot of a tree. Where you find one chanterelle, you are sure to find more.

Cantharellus cibarius (from the Greek word kantharos meaning a cup or goblet) is one of the most sought after of wild mushrooms, because of its wonderful apricot smell, its vivid egg yolk colour and its delicious flavour. The cap is wavy and bumpy and when the mushroom is fully grown it looks like a little umbrella which has blown inside out in a high wind. Its most distinguishing feature are its gills, which have been likened to the fan vaulting of a gothic cathedral. Somewhat unregimented, more like irregular folds or pin tucks than gills, they travel a little way down the stem ('decurrent' is the technical term) and merge with it, rather than stopping in a distinct line.

The only possible confusion is with the so-called false chanterelle (*Hygrophoropsis aurantiaca*), which is an even deeper orangey-yellow but very similar in almost all respects. Roger Phillips, in his book *Mushrooms*, describes the false chanterelle as 'said to be edible' but probably hallucinatory; in a German book I found it described as not dangerous, but not tasty either. The Larousse pocket guide to mushrooms (in French) scoffs at *ouvrages anciens* (old books) which give the mushroom as poisonous. 'It is nothing of the sort,' they claim. 'The false chanterelle is as good as the real one, and some people even prefer it.' I have neither found nor eaten the false chanterelle, so can't judge. As always with wild mushrooms, if in doubt, don't. (Or get an expert opinion from someone who knows, if you have that possibility.)

Chanterelles and beech trees go hand in hand – a happy accident for me, since we live surrounded by majestic and beautiful beech forests which are owned by our commune and accessible to all. (Often in Alsace there are signs on the trees saying that the gathering of *champignons* is outlawed, by order of the mayor; I asked him about this and he says it is designed to discourage non-residents. I took this as permission to forage.) In common with all mushrooms they like a good rainstorm after a nice warm spell. For some unlucky people, a change in the weather brings on a twinge of rheumatism; for me, it brings on that chanterelle feeling. I don my waterproofs, take a basket and a knife and set off into the woods. Sometimes I reflect ruefully that it would be wise to take a compass, or to drop a trail of pebbles along my way (à la Hansel and Gretel). The chase after chanterelles is an all-engrossing business and I regularly seem to get lost.

If you are lucky enough to find a batch of these wonderful fungi, lift them carefully from the forest floor, clean the feet and brush away any dirt or mossy bits. Once you've got them home, only brush them off under running water if they are very dirty; soaking is definitely not indicated. They will keep for a couple of days in the fridge wrapped in a damp teatowel sitting in a colander. If you have more than you can handle (a nice but unlikely prospect), blanch them and freeze them. Do not freeze them without blanching, or they turn bitter. They seem seldom to be sold dried, which

suggests to me that they don't dry well, though some books (and people) recommend it.

Chanterelles and eggs are a frequently found combination – indeed their German name *Eirschwamm*, often

expressed in the diminutive to indicate especial endearment – means 'little egg sponge'. Their apricot colour and aroma suggests an association with that fruit, which indeed works well. They also lend themselves to light white meats such as chicken breasts or diced veal or pork.

SALAD OF LOLLO WITH CHANTERELLES, APRICOTS AND WALNUTS

Lollo lettuce is arranged around the plate and the centre is filled with mushrooms, apricots, walnuts and herbs.

SERVES 4

100 ml / 3½ fl oz oil, of which a
    proportion could be walnut oil
2 tbsp vinegar
salt and pepper
1 tsp mustard
a pinch sugar
2 lollo rosso lettuces
200 g / 7 oz chanterelles

4 apricots, cut in eighths
1 tbsp chopped wild herbs: e.g.
    marjoram, thyme, and some
    herb flowers if available
2 tbsp herb vinegar (page 70) or
    balsamic vinegar
12 walnut halves

Make a dressing with all but 1 tbsp of the oil, the vinegar, salt, pepper, mustard and sugar. Separate the leaves of the lettuce, wash them and spin them dry. Cut away the base of each leaf so they will lie flat on the plate. Arrange them around 4 plates and sprinkle on some dressing. Slice or quarter the chanterelles, depending on size. Heat the reserved 1 tbsp oil with salt and pepper and fry the mushrooms for 6-7 minutes until their juice has evaporated. Add the apricot pieces and the herbs to the pan and fry briskly and very briefly. Sprinkle them warm over the lettuce leaves. Deglaze the pan with the herb or balsamic vinegar and sprinkle it on top. Garnish with the herb flowers and walnuts.

PAGLIA E FIENO WITH COURGETTES

Pale green and white pasta entwined with thin strips of courgette and topped with creamy orange mushrooms makes a special supper dish for 4, or a first course for 6.

SERVES 4-6

300 g / 10 oz paglia e fieno, or
    plain fine noodles
2 stock cubes
1 tbsp olive oil
1 clove garlic, crushed
2 small courgettes (US zucchini),
    pared with a potato peeler into

fine strips
200 g / 7 oz chanterelles, sliced
salt and pepper
1 tbsp finely chopped wild
    marjoram
200 ml / 7 fl oz whipping cream
    (US heavy cream)

Cook the pasta in plenty of boiling water with the stock cubes until just *al dente*. Toss the courgette strips in 1 tablespoon hot oil for about 5 minutes or until just limp. Add them to the hot pasta, turning to mix well. Keep these warm.

Fry the garlic in a little more oil, add the chanterelles, salt and pepper, cover and cook gently for 4-5 minutes. Uncover, raise the heat, sprinkle on the marjoram and cook till the juices are evaporated. Add the cream and simmer for a couple of minutes. Pour them over the pasta/courgettes and serve at once.

PAGLIA E FIENO WITH COURGETTES

ROLLED LOIN OF PORK
WITH CHANTERELLES AND APRICOTS

A boned roast of pork is marinated in lemon juice, honey and garlic, then seared in hot oil and gently cooked with dried apricots. Serve with ribbon noodles or polenta.

SERVES 6

a 1 kg / 2¼lb piece skinned and boned pork, rolled and tied	*75g / 2½oz dried apricots*
salt and pepper	*oil*
2 cloves garlic, crushed	*200g / 7oz chanterelles, sliced*
juice 1 lemon	*125 ml / 4 fl oz single cream (US light cream)*
1 tbsp runny honey	

Rub salt and pepper into the pork. Mix together the garlic, lemon juice and honey and spread it over the meat. Leave to marinate for a few hours in the fridge, or better still overnight. Cover the apricots with boiling water and leave for 10-15 minutes or until slightly plumped up.

Lift the meat out of the marinade and scrape away any pieces of garlic which cling to it. Reserve the marinade. Pat the meat dry with paper towels. Heat 1 tbsp oil in a heavy casserole with a lid and brown the meat on all sides.

Add the marinade and apricots to the casserole, cover with foil and lid and bake at 150°C / 300°F / Gas 2 for 45 minutes. Meanwhile fry the chanterelles in a little hot oil until the juices run. Raise the heat and cook hard to concentrate the juices. Season. Add the chanterelles to the pork and continue cooking for a further 15 minutes.

Remove the meat and keep it warm. Add the cream to the juices in the pan and boil hard to reduce by half. Remove the strings from the meat and slice it fairly thinly. Serve with the sauce.

SCRAMBLED EGGS WITH CHANTERELLES
AND WILD MARJORAM

When all the mushroom basket has yielded is a small handful of chanterelles, make them into this delicious supper dish.

SERVES 2

1 clove garlic, crushed	*salt and pepper*
1 tbsp olive oil	*2 sprigs wild marjoram in flower*
125g / 4½oz (about 12) chanterelles, sliced	*5 eggs*
	2 slices bread

Soften the garlic in the olive oil without allowing it to brown, then add the sliced mushrooms, salt, pepper and the finely chopped marjoram leaves. Cover and cook gently for 5 minutes. Uncover, raise the heat and cook briskly until the juices evaporate. Mix together the eggs, seasoned to taste, add them to the pan and scramble them gently – they should still be creamy. Pile on top of hot buttered toast and garnish with marjoram flowers.

CHERRY

PRUNUS AVIUM, P. CERASUS, P. PADUS

F: Cerisier des oiseaux, merisier; griotte.
G: Vogelkirsche, Wildkirsche.

What makes a cherry wild? (It sounds like a bad joke rather an attempt to define terms.) Beyond the obvious fact that the tree was not consciously planted where it is growing but probably sprang up from the chance dropping of a cherry-sated bird, things are somewhat unclear. 'Wild cherries are sour!' say some. But not all. The geans or mazzards (from the *Prunus avium* family) can be quite sweet if they've had enough sunshine. It is the pie or Morello cherries (*Prunus cerasus*) and the bird cherries (*P. padus*) which are sour. 'Wild cherries are black!' Some are, but others are red, or brownish, or even yellow. One thing is clear: they are very small – not much bigger than blackcurrants – and generally unrewarding to eat raw because in the ratio of flesh to stone, the dice are loaded in favour of the latter. On the other hand, they make outstanding jams, jellies, spirits, liqueurs and sauces. The answer is that if the tree is not obviously in someone's garden or orchard and its fruit is rather puny, you can take it that it's a wild cherry, or at least an escapee gone native.

For centuries, it was thought that the cherry tree originated in Asia Minor, and was brought to Italy and thence the rest of Europe from Pontus by the gourmet general Lucullus. Excavations of neolithic sites in various parts of Europe now show that some sort of wild cherry was native to the Continent. Probably the cherry which caught Lucullus' eye (or tickled his taste buds) was a fat, sweet cherry, which when crossed with the more northerly native wild fruit resulted in the succulent table cherries we know today.

Even today the wild cherry serves as grafting stock for cultivated fruit trees – though as is often the case when we try to 'improve' on nature, what we gain in size and flavour of the fruit, we lose in the health of the tree. Cultivated cherries are notoriously delicate and prone to disease, unlike their country cousins. The wood of the wild cherry has always been sought after by joiners and cabinetmakers and for use in decorative inlays or veneers. The bark is used in herbal medicine for persistent coughs, and a tea is made from cherry stalks, to be taken against diarrhoea and colds. In the old days in cherry-growing areas, the stones were packed into little hessian bags, which were warmed gently on top of old tiled stoves and used as bed warmers, or as little cushions (the bean bag principle) on which to lay tiny babies to prevent them rolling over. In some parts of Germany the tradition of the *Barbarazweige* lives on: a branch of wild cherry is cut around St Barbara's feast day (formerly 4 December) and brought into the house where, in the warmth of the *Stube*, it bursts into flower just in time for Christmas.

In this corner of Europe (known locally as the Regio, a term which includes Alsace, the Black Forest and northwest Switzerland), cherry trees – both wild and tamed – are a familiar part of the landscape. Wild cherries, which can achieve heights of more than 20 metres and live for a couple of hundred years, grow along roadsides, at the edge of woods and even deep in the forests. They flower a bit later than cultivated ones, which makes them less vulnerable to late frosts that can kill the crops; their fruit ripens during June and July. Picking wild cherries is a bothersome, messy and potentially dangerous business – the trees are very much higher than cultivated ones. It is little wonder (though rather sad) that hardly anyone bothers to pick them any more.

It is often thought that kirsch is distilled from wild cherries. In the old days, and on a domestic scale, this may have been so – even now, throughout the Regio where wild cherries are rife, some may find their way into the home still. But 'serious' kirsch, such as that made by the old family firm Schladerer in Staufen, is made from specially cultivated (and carefully tended) distilling cherries (known in German as *Brennkirschen*), chosen for their thin skins, copious juice, intense flavour and slightly bitter finish. A *Schwarzwälder Kirschwasser* may – in order to qualify for the appellation – contain only cherries grown in the Black Forest, and must be distilled in the area. Another extremely rare and wonderful kirsch is made by the Schladerers

from sour or Morello cherries: *Sauerkirschwasser*. And a proper Black Forest Cherry Cake worthy of the name is generously imbibed with kirsch and contains sour cherries (not sweet, canned ones or glacé cherries).

The best thing to do with wild cherries is to put them, along with other seasonal fruits, into a Rumpot. Beautiful decorated stoneware crocks are sold throughout our area for this purpose. The process starts in June with strawberries, then come the cherries and raspberries (wild and tame). In the middle some apricots slip in. Later come bilberries and in the autumn blackberries. Each time a new layer of fruit is added, sugar is sprinkled on and white rum (*rhum agricole* in France) is poured over to cover the fruit and exclude the air. The pot is covered with clingfilm and a lid. Over the months the fruit is nicely 'pickled' in a thoroughly alcoholic juice. Come Christmas time you can dip in and get thoroughly pickled yourself.

New Englanders for their part used to turn their native wild cherry (the so-called Rum Cherry, *P. serotina*) into a rum-based cherry liqueur, as well as an exciting sounding drink called Cherry Bounce, made with brandy on the sloe gin principle (page 155). Euell Gibbons, in *Stalking the Wild Asparagus*, relates that one New Englander decided, somewhat nervously, to make a present of some home-brandied cherries to the vicar of the parish. A charming thank-you note duly arrived, in which the minister thanked the parishioner not only for the gift itself but for the *spirit* in which it was given.

Sour Cherry Jam with Wild Cherries and Mint

Sour cherries combined with a handful of wild ones make a gorgeous jam. The sprigs of mint are optional but give a fresh and original touch. The sour cherries can be stoned, but leave the stones in the wild ones – some of them will float obligingly to the top and can be skimmed off before potting.

MAKES 4-5 JARS

1·5 kg / 3 lb 5 oz mixed cherries, of which at least 1 kg / 2¼ lb should be sour cherries

1 kg / 2¼ lb (US 5 cups) quick setting jam sugar with pectin

optional: 2 sprigs mint

Put the cherries in a preserving pan with the sugar and mint (if using) and leave them for about 2 hours or until the juice runs and the sugar starts to dissolve. Put a saucer in the freezer for testing the jam. Heat some jars in the oven.

Bring the cherries to boil and stir to dissolve the sugar completely. Count 5 minutes from when the jam started boiling, then start testing: put a little on the cold saucer and push a finger through it. A definite channel should form. If not, prolong the cooking a little.

Sweet-sour Wild Cherries

If you have access to plenty of wild cherries, make them into this delicious sweet-sour preserve for game, terrines or cold meats, which makes the most of their hedgerow flavour. As the cherries are usually too small to be stoned, you can leave the stones in – but warn people.

MAKES 1 LARGE OR 2 SMALL JARS

500 g / 1 lb 2 oz wild cherries
250 ml / 8 fl oz vinegar
250 ml / 8 fl oz red wine
200 g / 7 oz (US 1 cup) sugar
a 2 cm / ¾ inch piece cinnamon stick

1 tsp salt
2 cloves
a sprig winter savory
a piece orange zest

De-stalk and puncture the cherries in several places with a needle. Put them in a bowl. Bring to a boil the vinegar and wine, then add the sugar, cinnamon, salt, cloves, savory and orange zest. Simmer for 10 minutes. Pour it over the cherries and leave them for 24 hours in a cool place.

Next day, tip them into the pan and bring them to a simmer. Cook for about 10 minutes or until they begin to plump up. Lift them into the jar(s) with a slotted spoon and boil the juice down until reduced and somewhat syrupy. Pour it over the cherries, cover and keep for at least a month.

DUCK BREASTS WITH WILD CHERRY SAUCE

Wild cherries, sweet or sour, are simmered with stock, wine and spices, then reduced to give a sensational, sharp little sauce. Serve the duck with new potatoes and a courgette *Rösti* (page 62, omitting fat hen).

SERVES 6

1 shallot, finely chopped
50 g / scant 2 oz (US 3½ tbsp) butter
250 g / 9 oz wild cherries
1 tbsp kirsch
250 ml / 8 fl oz chicken stock, or water + ½ chicken stock cube
250 ml / 8 fl oz red wine
salt and pepper
a sprig thyme
4 duck breasts with skin: each weighing about 300 g / 10 oz
optional: juice ½ lemon
6 pairs of cherries on stalks to garnish

Make the sauce: soften the shallot in half of the butter, then add the cherries, kirsch, stock, wine, salt, pepper and thyme. Bring to the boil, cover and simmer for 10-15 minutes or until the cherries have split open. Lift them out with a slotted spoon and rub through a sieve. Discard the stones and the thyme. Return the liquid to the pan and boil down hard, to about a cupful. (Can be prepared ahead to this point and refrigerated or frozen.)

Score the skin of the duck breasts, season and barbecue them over fierce heat for 4-5 minutes each side, until still pink inside and the skin crusty; or put on a rack over a roasting pan with a little water in the bottom and grill (US broil) under a fierce heat until just done, turning once.

Reheat the sauce and whisk in the remaining butter cut in pieces. Sharpen if necessary with the lemon juice. Slice the duck thinly, splay the slices out over the sauce and garnish with a pair of cherries on stalks, if available.

BLACK FOREST CHERRY CAKE REVISITED

Most Black Forest cakes are beastly. The sponge cake is boring, and tastes more of cardboard than of chocolate; there's too much whipped cream; and the cherries come out of a can. Here is my version: a seriously dark chocolate-almond sponge laced with kirsch and filled with sharp cherries and whipped cream. Serve extra cherries in brandy to accompany if you wish.

MAKES A CAKE SERVING 4-6 PEOPLE

75g / 2¹/₂oz best-quality dark chocolate
1 tbsp water
50g / scant 2oz (US 3¹/₂tbsp) unsalted butter
3 eggs, separated
50g / scant 2oz (US ²/₃ cup) ground almonds or hazelnuts
1 tbsp kirsch or Schladerer Sauerkirschwasser

a pinch salt
40g / scant 1¹/₂oz (US 3 tbsp) sugar
150g / 5oz brandied wild cherries (page 55) plus 4 tbsp brandy from the cherries
125ml / 4floz whipped cream
icing sugar (US confectioners' sugar

Heat the oven to 180°C / 350°F / Gas 4.

Butter and flour the sides of an 18cm / 7¹/₄ inch springform cake pan and put a disc of non-stick paper in the bottom.

Break up the chocolate and melt it over very gentle heat in a heavy-based pan with the water. Stir until smooth and glossy, then remove from the heat and stir in the butter, cut in small pieces, and the egg yolks. Stir in the ground nuts and kirsch. The mixture will be thick.

Beat the egg whites with the salt into soft peaks. Add the sugar and continue beating until the consistency of meringue. Fold into the chocolate-nut mixture. Scoop into the prepared pan and bake in the preheated oven for 35-40 minutes or until risen and just firm. Remove from the oven, release the springform and cool the cake on a rack.

Split the cake in two layers and spoon the brandy from the cherries over the two layers. Fold the cherries into the lightly sweetened whipped cream and spread them over one of the cake layers. Reassemble and chill the cake. To serve, sprinkle with icing sugar and arrange a few cherries on top (with stalks, if available).

BRANDIED WILD CHERRIES

The original recipe for these, from a Dutch neighbour, calls for sour cherries, but wild cherries, with their thin flesh and wonderful flavour, work well too – or use a combination. Made in July, they should be nicely matured by Christmas: use them spooned over ice cream, either cold or hot, for a quick and easy dessert to lift the spirits.

MAKES 1 LITRE / 1²/₃ PINTS (US 1 QUART)

1 kg / 2¹/₄lb cherries: sour and/or wild
1 litre 1²/₃ pints (US 1 quart) colourless, tasteless grape

brandy
1 kg / 2¹/₄lb (US 5 cups) sugar
a cinnamon stick

Prick the cherries all over and put them in a glass jar with a tight-fitting lid. Add the brandy, sugar and cinnamon stick. Close tightly and hide them away until Christmas. Gyrate the jar gently now and then to dissolve the sugar.

ELDER

SAMBUCUS NIGRA

F: Sureau. G: Holunder. Wander along a country lane or along the banks of a stream in early summer and the air will be thick with the heady scent of elderflowers. It is the elder tree's big moment. An otherwise unremarkable specimen during the rest of the year, it is suddenly decked from head to toe with frothy white flowerheads like lace mob caps.

Elders do not have delusions of grandeur and are content to grow in forgotten corners of farmyards, in dilapidated gardens, in hedges and ditches, beside rivers and streams and often in graveyards. My own favourite grows up against the old bunker on the Maginot Line up above our village.

Of all the old-established wild trees, the elder has perhaps the greatest number of superstitions and traditions associated with it. In old-fashioned children's story books (the sort which provoked a delicious shiver of fear and would be proscribed nowadays) it was the elder tree which incorporated in its branches a craggy old face and tousled hair – now you saw it, now you didn't. The image, though spooky, was meant kindly enough, for the spirit which lived in the tree was supposed to frighten away other less benign spirits, to whisper advice into the wind through its rustling leaves, and to shelter and care for those sitting in its grateful shade. According to legend, the elder tree was never struck by lightning, a belief which may have had its roots in pagan traditions, or in the later Christian belief that the cross on which Jesus was crucified was said to have been made from elder.

Sticks cut from the branches of the elder tree were variously employed: the Sicilians used them for killing snakes and driving away robbers, the Serbs in their wedding ceremonies to bring happiness to the bridal pair, the English as a talisman in the pocket to protect against rheumatism. Country children in Alsace (according to Marguerite Doerflinger in *Toute la Gastronomie Alsacienne*), being of a more practical turn of mind, hollowed them out to make water pistols, whistles, pea-shooters or drinking straws.

Elder leaves have an unpleasant smell and were used (indeed still are, by some organic gardeners) in a decoction as an insect repellent. In the old days, the branches were hung outside cowsheds to keep away the flies, or tucked inside the hat as a variant on the Australian's bobbing corks. In some places the elder is known as the badger's herb: the tree is often to be found growing near badger setts and it seems that the animals strew the leaves on the floor of the setts to make (it is supposed) an insect-repellent carpet.

Elderflowers are the tree's crowning summer glory (as distinct from the berries, which are a bit of an autumn disappointment) and can be used in many different ways. Pick them on a dry day, with a weather eye for black aphids which can infest the stalks. Snip the flowers off the stalks (which have the same unpleasantly rank smell as the leaves). They can be used in syrups, pancakes, crêpes, ice creams and *crèmes anglaises*. Stew some flowers in with a breakfast compote of rhubarb, sweetened to taste. Or macerate a handful in a flask of good wine vinegar, then strain (see herb vinegars, page 70) and bottle. Use a splash when making meringues to give a soft, marshmallow-like texture and a little hint of elderflower, or to deglaze pans, or in dressings.

One of the most traditional ways of using elder-flowers (or indeed acacia blossoms, which appear at the same time) is to make them into fritters: the flowers are left on the stalk, dunked in a light batter (made in these parts with the addition of beer for extra lightness), deep fried and dusted with sugar. The lightly crusted golden flowers are then nibbled off the stalks. The flowers were also used medicinally: said to stimulate sweating, they were prescribed for feeding fevers, either in the form of syrups or tisanes (the latter often combined with lime-flowers, which bloom concurrently).

By the time autumn comes, that profusion of creamy-white flowers has turned into an abundance of little black berries. Gone is the magic fragrance of June; all that is left is a cloying sweetness and a starchy consistency. Some people make a reputedly delicious jelly from the berries, combined with crab or sharp apples. Somewhere I read that you can make them into a hair dye – which may be the best use for them. Beware though: it seems that the black dye they contain is as effective on the scalp as it is on the hair, and results may be unexpectedly comprehensive.

SPEEDY STRAWBERRY AND ELDERFLOWER JAM

A quick and easy conserve which should not be kept too long as the cooking is minimal and the sugar content rather low.

MAKES 7-8 JARS

2 kg / 4¹/₂lb strawberries, hulled and halved or quartered	plucked off stalks
4 heads of elderflower, flowers	1 kg / 2¹/₄lb quick-setting jam sugar with added pectin

Put the strawberries in a preserving pan with the elder-flowers. Follow the instructions on the packet of preserving sugar on how and when to add. Cook as directed until setting point is reached. Pull to one side and leave for 5-10 minutes. Then stir to redistribute the fruit. Pour into hot jars, label and store. Keep refrigerated once opened.

ELDERFLOWER SYRUP

This wonderful summer drink, nicely sharpened by the lemon and citric acid, captures all the elusive and haunting flavour of elderflowers. Use it simply as a thirst-slaking drink during the summer months, or to perfume summer puddings, fruit salads or mousses. You can boil the syrup after straining it, but you lose some of the flavour and all of the vitamins. If not boiled, it sometimes ferments a little in the bottle, so do not cork it too tightly or you may have an explosive situation.

MAKES ABOUT 2 LITRES/3½ PINTS (US 2 QUARTS)

30 elderflower heads
2 litres/3½ pints (US 2 quarts) water
1·5kg/3lb 5oz (US 7½ cups) sugar
50g/1¾oz citric acid crystals
juice 2 lemons

If the elderflowers were picked just after the rain, spread them out on a teatowel to dry for a few hours, otherwise yeasts can grow on them and produce mould in the finished syrup. Put them in a large bowl. Bring the water and sugar to the boil, stirring occasionally to ensure the sugar dissolves. Remove from the heat, add the citric acid crystals and lemon juice, and pour this over the flowers. They will go rather a murky colour. Cool, then cover and leave to infuse for about 5 days in a cool place.

Strain the syrup roughly through a colander. Discard the flowers. Strain the syrup once more through a nappy or diaper liner, muslin or cheesecloth. Bottle the syrup. Cork it not too tightly or use old-fashioned 'pop' bottles with a hinged stopper. Keep in the fridge and dilute as for orange squash or other drink concentrates.

ELDERFLOWER CRÈME ANGLAISE

Instead of infusing your milk for *crème anglaise* with vanilla, use some heads of elderflower. It makes a wonderful ice cream base, or a sauce for fresh fruit, meringue and other desserts.

MAKES 500 ML/16 FL OZ

500ml/16floz milk
6 heads of elderflower, trimmed off the stalks: about 10-15g/⅔-½oz
4 egg yolks
100g/3½oz (US ½ cup) sugar

Bring the milk to a boil, drop in the elderflowers, remove from the heat, cover and leave to infuse for 1 hour. Strain the milk and reheat to just under the boil. Beat together the yolks and sugar and pour on the hot milk. Return the mixture to the pan and stir vigorously with a wire whisk over gentle heat until wisps of steam start to rise. Dip a spoon into the custard, then draw your finger down the back of it: a definite channel should form. The custard should be about the consistency of single (thin) cream. (Do not let it boil or you will have scrambled eggs *aux fleurs de sureau*.) Snatch it from the fire and pour it into a bowl, to prevent further cooking. Cool the custard, then cover with clingfilm and chill.

ICED MERINGUE SANDWICHES WITH ELDERFLOWER CRÈME ANGLAISE

Making *crème anglaise* always leaves you with a glut of egg whites. Whip them up into these meringues, sandwich them with raspberry or blackcurrant sorbet (it should be something sharp and colourful for contrast) and freeze them ready for a dinner party.

SERVES 6

4 egg whites
a pinch salt
200g / 7oz (US 1 cup) sugar
2 tsp cornflour (US cornstarch)
1 tbsp vinegar
optional: 3-4 tbsp flaked almonds
    (US sliced almonds)

raspberry or blackcurrant sorbet
elderflower crème anglaise (see
    page 58)
fresh berries to garnish

Heat the oven to 100°C / 212°F / Gas $\frac{1}{4}$. Draw 12 discs each 12 cm/5 inches diameter on 2 sheets of non-stick baking paper which will fit on 2 baking sheets.

Beat the whites with the salt until snowy. Add the sugar and cornflour and continue beating until stiff and glossy. Whisk in the vinegar. Divide the mixture among the discs drawn on the paper, spreading it out smoothly to the edges to make neat circles. If using flaked almonds, scatter them over half the meringue discs. Bake them in the pre-heated oven for about 1 hour or until they will lift off the paper without sticking.

Allow the sorbet to soften to a malleable consistency, then use to sandwich the meringue discs in pairs (almond sides uppermost, if you have used them) and freeze them. Serve one per person, set over the elderflower sauce, and garnish with berries and/or elderflower sprigs.

MOUSSES OF FROMAGE FRAIS WITH ELDERFLOWER

These mousses make an excellent ending to a rich meal: lightly set mounds of *fromage frais* or Greek yogurt flavoured with elderflowers are turned out over a fruit coulis and served with fresh fruit. If you have no home-made syrup, use bottled elderflower cordial or pressé.

SERVES 6

2 tsp powdered unflavoured
    gelatine or 4 sheets gelatine
150 ml / 5 fl oz elderflower syrup
    (page 58) or elderflower
    cordial
500 ml / 16 fl oz fromage frais or
Greek yogurt

100 ml / 3½ fl oz whipping cream
    (US heavy cream)
500 g / 1 lb 2oz red fruit:
    strawberries, raspberries,
    redcurrants or a mixture

If using powdered gelatine, sprinkle it on to 6 tbsp elder-flower syrup (or cordial) and leave until spongy. Then dissolve it over gentle heat. If using sheet gelatine, soak it in cold water until floppy. Squeeze out the sheets and dissolve them in 6 tbsp of the elderflower syrup or cordial.

Put the *fromage frais* or Greek yogurt in the food processor or blender, turn on the motor and pour in the warm gelatine. Process or blend until smooth. Whip the cream to soft peaks and fold it into the mixture. Lightly oil six 125 ml / 4 fl oz ramekins and divide the mixture among them. Leave in the fridge for about 4 hours or until set.

Set aside some fruit to garnish the mousses. Purée the rest with the remaining elderflower syrup or cordial. Sieve to eliminate seeds. Loosen to a pouring consistency if necessary with a little water (or more elderflower syrup). Serve with the mousses.

FAT HEN

CHENOPODIUM ALBUM

F: Chénopode blanc. G: Weiße Chenopodium. You probably know fat hen better than you think. An annual plant, it is an extremely common weed which grows in newly tilled soil, on building sites and bomb sites. When we moved into our newly built house (easily mistaken for a bomb site at the time) and started to clear the ground to make a garden, it sprang up everywhere. For a while it irritated me. When I discovered it was delicious to eat, my feelings towards it warmed and my weekly weeding task took on quite another dimension.

Fat hen belongs to the chenopodium family which derives its name from the Greek *chen* (goose) and *pous, podos* (foot). Study the web-foot-like formation of the leaves of any of the clan and you can readily see where its name comes from. Among fat hen's siblings are Good King Henry (*Chenopodium bonus-henricus*) and *epazote* (*C. ambrosioides*), the pungent Mexican herb essential for brewing up a good pot of beans. More distant relatives are orache or mountain spinach (*C. atriplex*) and New Zealand spinach (*C. tetragonia*).

Fat hen is my favourite chenopode. Also known as goosefoot or wild spinach, it is just as delicious as spinach and has the inestimable advantage of growing steadily throughout the hot summer months when successive sowings of garden spinach have long since tiresomely bolted. Its web-footed leaves are of a dull green shade, and curiously mealy. After a thunderstorm, residual raindrops sit fatly on their upturned surface, rather as they do on the leaves of lady's mantle.

Perhaps this accounts, by association, for another of the plant's familiar names: mercury. By the end of summer – if you haven't rooted it out by now – the plant will have grown up to about a metre. The leaves grow all the way up the stem, initially off the main slender stalk, and gradually forming their own little branchlets until the plant turns into a veritable little bush encrusted with tiny, pimple-like flowers. Later these develop into seeds which are liberally scattered around the countryside. Since it has been estimated that the seeds of fat hen make up about half of the entire population of weed seeds to be found in the soils of the whole of central Europe, you can rest assured that there will never be any shortage of this delicious piece of greenery.

For harvesting, however, it is best to pick the plant when still only about 20 cm/8 inches high. Strip off all the leaves and discard the stalks. Wash well and use immediately. Any recipe involving spinach can be re-interpreted to accommodate fat hen.

FAT HEN TIMBALES WITH CHANTERELLES

Little green custards of fat hen are turned out and sur-rounded with garlicky chanterelles. The slightly crunchy orange mushrooms make an appealing contrast with the smooth green of the vegetable timbales.

SERVES 4

AS A STARTER

about 30 stalks fat hen: to give
  2 handfuls when stripped off
  stalks, or around 100g / 3$^{1}/_{2}$oz
3 eggs
250ml / 8floz + about 4tbsp
  whipping cream (US heavy
  cream)
salt and pepper

1 shallot, finely chopped
1 clove garlic, crushed
12g / scant $^{1}/_{2}$oz (US 1tbsp)
  butter
400g / 14oz chanterelles, cleaned
  and sliced
sprigs of chervil

Wash the fat hen leaves and put in a pan with only the water which clings to them. Cook over high heat for 4-5 minutes or until still brilliant green and slightly limp. Drain off any water. Put in the blender or food processor with the eggs, 250ml / 8floz cream, and salt and pepper to taste. Purée until smooth.

Heat the oven to 180°C / 350°F / Gas 4. Butter four 125ml / 4floz ramekins and put a disc of non-stick paper in the bottom. Pour in the custard. Put the ramekins in a roasting pan with water two-thirds of the way up the sides. Bring the water to a simmer on top of the stove, then bake for 25-30 minutes or until firm and slightly risen.

Meanwhile, soften the shallot and garlic in the butter and oil until tender but not brown. Add the sliced chanterelles and salt and pepper to taste. Cover and cook for 7-8 minutes until the juices run. Uncover the pan and cook a further 5-6 minutes until the juices evaporate. Remove from the heat and stir in 4 tbsp cream. Remove the timbales from the oven, turn out on to heated plates and peel off the paper. Spoon the chanterelles around the timbales and put a sprig of chervil on top.

FAT HEN RISOTTO WITH SMOKED FISH

A tasty supper dish to be made with cut-offs from a side of smoked salmon, or other smoked fish.

SERVES 4

about 30 stalks fat hen: to give
  2 handfuls when stripped off
  stalks, or around 100g / 3$^{1}/_{2}$oz
900ml-1·2 litres / 1$^{1}/_{2}$-2 pints
  (US 4-5 cups) chicken stock,
  or water + 2 chicken stock
  cubes
1 onion, finely chopped

1 clove garlic, mashed
1 tbsp oil
350g / 12 oz (US 1$^{1}/_{2}$ cups)
  Aroborio or Vialone rice
200g / 7oz smoked salmon, or
  smoked trout, mackerel, kippers
  etc, cut in thin strips

Cook the fat hen in boiling salted water for 5 minutes. Drain and refresh in cold water to set the colour. Purée in a blender or food processor with some stock till smooth.

Soften the onion and garlic gently in the oil, then add the rice and cook for about 5 minutes, stirring constantly. Add the stock bit by bit, cooking over moderate heat; wait until the stock is absorbed, then add more. When 900ml / 1$^{1}/_{2}$ pints (US just under 4 cups) has been added, taste the rice; it should be cooked (al dente) and still creamy – add more stock if necessary. Stir in the fat hen purée and smoked fish and cook for 5 minutes more.

COURGETTE AND FAT HEN RÖSTI

Fat hen leaves are lightly cooked, mixed with grated courgettes and eggs and fried in hot oil. Serve with cold meats for supper, or on its own as a vegetarian dish. A spicy fresh tomato sauce (see page 78) could also be served.

SERVES 4

2 large courgettes (US zucchini): about 400g/14oz
salt
2 good handfuls fat hen, leaves stripped off stalks to give about 100g/3½oz
2 eggs

finely chopped herbs of your choice
1 spring onion (US scallion), finely chopped
2 tbsp flour
oil

Grate the courgettes on a coarse grater or the grating disc of the food processor. Put them in a colander and sprinkle with salt. Leave to drain.

Cook the fat hen in boiling salted water for 5 minutes. Drain, refresh in cold water and squeeze dry. Chop it roughly, or put it in the food processor. Process or mix together with the eggs, herbs, spring onion and flour. Squeeze out the courgettes and stir them into the mixture. Heat a film of oil in a non-stick frying pan. Pour in the courgette mixture and cook over steady heat until the underside is brown and the *Rösti* just firm, not wobbly. Invert a plate over it and turn it out. Heat a little more oil in the pan and slide the *Rösti* back into the pan to cook the underside.

FINE NOODLES WITH FAT HEN AND QUAIL'S EGGS

An excellent supper dish: a nest of fine pasta is filled with quail's eggs and sprinkled with bacon dice, served over a creamy fat hen sauce.

SERVES 4

20-30 stalks fat hen, to give about 100g/3½oz leaves stripped off stalks
250ml/8floz single or whipping cream (US light or heavy cream)
salt and pepper
nutmeg

350g/12oz fresh pasta: fine noodles, tagliatelle, paglia e fieno etc
150g/5oz streaky bacon, diced small
12 quail's eggs, boiled 3 minutes, drained, refreshed in cold water and peeled

Cook the fat hen in boiling salted water for 5 minutes. Drain and refresh in cold water to set the colour. Squeeze it out and chop it roughly. Put in the blender with the cream, salt, pepper and nutmeg and blend till quite smooth. Return it to the pan.

Cook the pasta until *al dente*. Fry the bacon bits without extra fat until golden and crispy; drain them on absorbent paper. Heat the sauce just to boiling and divide it among 4 heated plates. Put the pasta on top in a nest formation. Arrange 3 eggs per person in the 'nests' and sprinkle the bacon bits on top.

FINE NOODLES WITH FAT HEN AND QUAIL'S EGGS

HERBS

For people who live in temperate lands, where herbs are confined to the chill-cabinet of the supermarket or packed (dry and dusty) into small jars, there is little to match the excitement of coming upon wild herbs, free for the picking. Take an early morning walk in the *garrigue*, the scrubby, scorched hinterland of the Mediterranean, and within the space of a few minutes you will have trodden underfoot half a dozen familiar herbs and brushed past two or three more: thyme, sage and savory, rosemary bushes thick with pale blue flowers, fennel waving its feathery heads. Even the bay tree grows wild.

Pick a bunch or two of wild herbs, bundle them up and bear them back home. Hang them in a dry, warm place out of direct sunlight and they will dry beautifully and keep quite a bit of their flavour and colour. Later in the year they will remind you of long, hot summer days when the foods which appealed most were cool salads sprinkled with dismantled thyme flowers, barbecued fish with fennel, tiny lamb chops or poussins marinated in mountain savory or rosemary oil. And even if you can't migrate southwards during the summer months, there is still mint and lemon balm, marjoram and wild thyme to comfort you in cooler climes. Besides their multiple uses both fresh and dried, in cooking as in garnishes, wild herbs make wonderful potpourri and herb garlands.

To find **thyme** (*Thymus spp.*, thyme, Thymian) growing in wild profusion always gives me a particular thrill: where I live, my treasured thyme bush is lucky to survive the Alsace winter, even in the shelter of the herb garden. In the arid regions of southern Europe, common (or garden) thyme, *Thymus vulgaris*, grows wild; still more widespread, growing on grassy banks and lime-

THYME

stone soils, is the small, wiry, creeping variety, the so-called wild thyme or serpolet (*Thymus serpyllum*). Both sorts have tiny pinkish-mauve flowerheads and are best gathered in full bloom when the plant is at its most fragrant.

Be careful when picking wild thyme, which is all too easily uprooted. The characteristically pungent essential oils contained in the herb are stronger in common than in wild thyme, so generous measures are called for in your use of the latter. The flowers make a most beautiful garnish for summer salads or grilled meats.

Wild thyme has been valued for centuries, even more for medicinal than for culinary purposes. The ancient Egyptians used it for embalming corpses, while the Greeks considered that it brought courage and wore sprigs of it in their helmets before going to war (the name thyme apparently derives from the Greek word meaning valour). The bravery theme was sustained over many centuries and among different peoples: Roman soldiers girded their loins before battle with fragrant baths of thyme, while medieval English ladies embroidered thyme motifs on the handkerchiefs of their knights errant. The antiseptic and preservative properties valued by the Egyptian embalmers were later put to good use in the kitchen: in pre-refrigerator days, the use of thyme in stuffings for poultry and meats may have been more of a precaution than a flavouring.

The average northerly bush of garden **rosemary** (*Rosmarinus officinalis*, romarin, Rosmarin) seems a polite and sober affair compared with the rampant rosemary which tumbles wild over the dry stone walls of Mediterranean vineyards, and grows into great bushes on windswept, sunbaked hillsides. The air all around is thick with its scent, you don't have to pinch it or push

ROSEMARY

it, or even cook it, its essential oils are released simply by the relentless heat of the sun.

Throughout the ages people have valued rosemary as an aid to failing memory. From being a herb to cure forgetfulness, it was transposed and became the herb of remembrance (hence its presence at funerals), of fidelity between spouses (ditto at weddings) and loyalty amongst friends. Sir Thomas More wrote of it: 'I lette it run all over my garden walls, not onlie because my bees love it, but because it is the herb sacred to remembrance and to friendship, whence a sprig of it hath a dumb-language.'

If you have picked plenty of branches in the wild, strip the spiky leaves off the branches and dry and store them. Whittle the twigs down smoothly and use them as skewers for kebabs. Besides all its traditional tried and tested uses, rosemary makes a particularly well-flavoured herb oil (page 70), a useful adjunct to summer marinades.

Sage (*Salvia officinalis*, sauge, Salbei), the sacred herb of the Romans, is another sun-worshipper which seems able to thrive in the poorest soils and with the minimum of water. Originally a native of the wild Dalmatian coast, its silver-grey leaves vary in size from diminutive to long and lobe-like. Its prawn-like flowers have a pinkish exterior at first, later opening to reveal rich blue petals.

SAGE

This elegant herb has always been regarded as a lifesaving and -enhancing plant (the name has the same root as 'salvation'). Louis XIV is said to have taken a daily infusion of sage and veronica in the misguided belief that it would make him immortal.

The related meadow clary, *Salvia pratensis*, is hardier and grows further north. Its startlingly blue blooms appear on tall slender stalks on roadsides and in the meadows just before the hay is cut. Clary sage, *Salvia sclarea*, with handsome pinkish-mauve flowers, is different again; in Germany it is known as *Muskateller-Salbei* because of its supposed muscat aroma, while in some countries it was used by brewers to give an extra kick to their beer. The use of both meadow clary and clary sage to clear up eye infections dates back many centuries. Both were in common culinary use, but their use in the contemporary kitchen is limited because of scarcity.

Sage, like rosemary, should be

used sparingly and singly. In England roast turkey without sage in the stuffing would be unthinkable, but its use other than with pork is fairly limited. The Italians are a bit more adventurous and use the herb with pasta, with liver and with veal. It is the principal flavouring in the curious Provençal *aigo bouillido*, a cross between a restorative soup and a soothing tisane based loosely on water, plenty of garlic and olive oil. The herb's digestive properties are well-known: in some areas, sage leaves and/or flowers are infused in brandy to give a postprandial liqueur. Try using sage leaves to infuse an apple-based jelly, for serving with cold meats (see page 72) or to give a sweetly herbal finish to a sauce for pork or white meats. Both leaves and flowers can be steeped in oil to give a fragrant and beautiful lubricant for barbecued or roasted meats. (See herb oil, page 70.)

WINTER SAVORY

Throughout southern parts of Europe, great bushes of shrubby, evergreen **winter savory** (*Satureja montana*, sarriette, Bohnenkraut) perfume the arid hillsides. (Summer savory, *Satureja hortensis*, is a commonly cultivated annual which self-seeds itself in the wild, and whose culinary uses are similar.) Virgil suggested siting the plant near beehives, a sound idea on two counts: it is an excellent source of nectar for the bees, as well as a time-honoured remedy in case of bee stings. The *satureja* part of the name is thought to come from the Latin meaning satyr, and the herb has always enjoyed a somewhat racy reputation – such was its fame as an aphrodisiac that it was banned from medieval monastery gardens, for fear of stimulating desires considered inappropriate to the celibate life.

In German its name means 'bean-herb' – certainly its peppery nature combined with its digestive effect makes it a good partner for all kinds of beans, whether French, runner, broad or (especially) dried, and for pulses and legumes of any sort. Because of its robust, spicy character, it also goes well with game. It should never be chopped or it will become bitter: simply strip the spikes from the stalks, rub them gently between your fingers and scatter them over the chosen dish.

Fennel (*Foeniculum vulgare*, fenouil, Fenchel) is another child of the sun which grows wild all around the Mediterranean. A biennial, it readily reproduces itself from the numerous seeds borne high on the plant. The tall green bendy stalks are clothed with feathery leaves and culminate in inverted umbrellas of yellow flowers. All parts of the herb, which has a pronounced aniseed flavour, are extensively used in southern cookery.

While rosemary was reputed to restore memory and sage to ensure long life, fennel was supposed to help with failing eyesight. A popularly held belief, related by Pliny amongst others, was that serpents, as they cast their skin, would roll in branches of fennel (or drink the juice, or even rub it into their eyes, depending on the story) in order to sharpen their vision. Thanks to the Romans, the plant soon spread throughout the Mediterranean area and in due course to the monastery gardens of the rest of Europe. It has also acquired a reputation as a slimming aid, perhaps because it is thought to

FENNEL

help in the digestion of fatty foods: a sixteenth-century text suggests 'seething fennel in water … for to make one slender'.

Fish needs fennel; but so do many other foods, especially light white meats and summer vegetables. A whole salmon brushed with oil, filled to bursting with fennel and put straight on to the bars of a barbecue, is a summer treat to remember. Any vegetables cooked *à la grecque* benefit from a good bunch of the herb or a little pinch of seeds.

In cooler climes, **lemon balm** (*Melissa officinalis*, mélisse, Zitronenmelisse) grows very freely, often becoming a rather tiresome weed. A medium-sized, nettle-like plant which forms pleasing-shaped clumps, it is a magnet for bees (*Melissa* comes from the Greek word meaning bee).

Though this herb enjoys the label *officinalis* (meaning 'of medicinal use'), its therapeutic value is vague. Most often it is made into an infusion, and seems to have been appreciated as long ago as the tenth century by Arab physicians who prescribed it for melancholy. More recently a (male?) French *phytotherapeute* recommended it for treating 'attacks of bad humour in young girls and feeble women'.

Its pleasant lemony flavour makes it a good addition to salads, chopped over at the last minute as the flavour quickly fades. It makes an excellent herb vinegar (page 70). One of the best ways of using it is to stir some into an apple-based jelly (see herb jelly, page 72).

LEMON BALM

Wild marjoram or **oregano** (*Origanum vulgare*, origan commun, Dost) – not to be confused with sweet marjoram, *Origanum majorana* (marjolaine, Majoran) – is found in the wild throughout most of Europe. It likes sunny, well-exposed banks and hillsides, and its flowers – mauve or purple mopheads which dry beautifully and keep their colour and fragrance – are borne profusely throughout high summer. The hotter the climate, the more fragrant the herb: the wild marjoram which I pick from the roadsides of southern Alsace is a good deal less pungent than that which we found growing along the banks of the Canal du Midi. The leaves can be stripped off the plant and used fresh or dried. The stems are reddish and quite tough and should not be used.

This beautiful herb seems always to have been associated with joy. A tea of wild marjoram

MARJORAM

was recommended by the English herbalist Gerard for those 'given to overmuch sighing'. I find it a great spirit-lifter, not only because of its gorgeous flavour, but because of the luxuriant beauty of its purple flowers, always buzzing with bees and butterflies. The flowers make wonderful herb garlands, woven in with sage leaves, sprigs of rosemary and bay leaves.

There are as many varieties of **mint** (*Mentha spp.*, menthe, Minze) as sparks in Vulcan's furnace, claimed a medieval monk. Plenty of them grow wild, notably corn mint (*Mentha arvensis*), a pale green variety which grows in pastures and whose pink flowers grow off the stems at the junction with the leaves); water mint (*M. aquatica*), a beautiful, sometimes slightly bronze-leafed plant which thrives beside streams and in damp places and whose rounded flowers are borne at the top of the stem; and horse mint (*M. longifolia*), a tall hedgerow plant with elongated pink flowers at the tip of each long stem.

The name mint is said to come from Mintha, the Greek name of a nymph who was turned into a plant by Persephone, in a fit of pique. Wild mints may be used interchangeably with garden mints, though you should taste them first as some are extremely pungent and should be used with caution. While mint is beloved by the British for their mint sauces and jellies, the French are appalled at the idea of using it in

conjunction with vinegar and sugar to season lamb, and prefer to use it in tisanes. It is extensively used in Arab and in Greek cookery in salads and lamb dishes. Add a little chopped mint to creamy dressing (page 6) and pour it over cooked, cooled, peeled new potatoes.

MINT

WILD HERB BUTTER

Using the system described on page 35 for wild garlic butter, and substituting wild herbs for wild garlic (alone or in combination), you can make wild herb butters for use with barbecued or roasted meats, or for sliding between the slices of a French loaf. Wrap the bread in foil and heat in the oven until crisp and the butter has melted.

WILD HERB OIL

Here is a fine way of capturing the summer fragrance of wild herbs for uncapping in the dark, dreary months of winter. You can make a mixed herb oil, or concentrate on one herb alone. If wished, a sprig of some fresh herb, preferably in flower (marjoram or thyme look especially nice), can be put into the bottles before pouring in the oil.

**MAKES ABOUT 1·5 LITRES/2½ PINTS
(US 1½ QUARTS)**

*chosen wild herb(s), flowering if
    you wish
optional: 4 cloves garlic, peeled
    and bruised*

*500 ml / 16 fl oz olive oil
1 litre / 1⅔ pints (US 1 quart)
    tasteless salad oil*

Do not wash the herbs unless mud-splashed. If you must wash them, be sure they are dry before you put them in the jar with the oil, otherwise it will become cloudy. Loosely pack them into some large Kilner or jam jars with tight fitting lids. Add the garlic if using and pour over the mixture of olive and salad oil to cover the herbs completely. Cover and leave in a dark, cool place for at least a month, turning gently once in a while.

Once the oil is well flavoured, strain through a colander into a large jug. Strain it again through muslin and pour into clean, dry, clear bottles. (I use glass tonic water bottles, or clear tall Alsace wine bottles, depending on the size I want, and cork them with wine bottle corks.)

Favourites: sage oil (for basting meats, especially pork); fennel oil (for fish on the barbecue); savory oil (drizzle over cooked beans); rosemary oil (for lamb); wild marjoram oil (for salads, especially tomato); 'Scarborough Fair' oil: parsley, sage, rosemary and thyme (for any meats).

WILD HERB VINEGAR

The same system applies as for making herb oil except that the vinegar should be left on a sunny windowsill (rather than in the dark) to extract maximum flavour. Cover the chosen herb(s) with white wine or cider vinegar, add 2 or 3 peeled, bruised cloves of garlic (optional) and leave to macerate for 1-2 months. Strain, filter and decant as above. Use herb vinegars for deglazing pans after frying meat or fish, as well as for original salad dressings.

Special favourites: mint vinegar (for vinaigrette for cucumber salad, or a creamy dressing for potato salad); lemon balm vinegar (for vinaigrette, any salad); thyme vinegar (a 'passe-partout' vinegar); wild marjoram vinegar (ditto); wild garlic vinegar.

GOAT'S CHEESES MARINATED IN OIL WITH HERBS AND GARLIC

Even those who think they hate goat's cheese risk being converted by this. Take some tiny fresh goat's cheeses (e.g. *Chevretines*) or cut a goat log (*buche de chèvre*) in slices. Put them in a jar into which they will just fit. Slide some herb sprigs (thyme, savory or rosemary work particularly well) down the side of the jar and fill up with olive oil. Label and date them, and store in the fridge for at least a month before using. They will keep for longer, given the chance, getting ever more pungent the longer you leave them.

WILD HERB OIL

WILD HERB JELLY

Herb jellies (made on an apple base) are lovely with all sorts of meats, hot or cold – thyme or lemon balm jelly with cold chicken, for instance, or the more classic mint jelly with lamb. Or you can stir a tablespoonful into a finished sauce or gravy to give it a nice piquancy. A selection of jellies, vinegars and oils in a box make an attractive Christmas present.

MAKES 4-5 SMALL JARS

2 kg / 4¹/₂ lb apples, roughly chopped
1·5-2 litres / 2¹/₃-3¹/₂ pints (US 1¹/₂-2 quarts) water
700 g / 1 lb 9 oz (US 3¹/₂ cups) sugar

juice 2 lemons, or 100 ml / 3¹/₂ fl oz wine vinegar
chosen herb (see recipe)

Do not peel or core the apples. Simply cut away any bruised or unsavoury bits, then quarter and chop them roughly. Put them in a preserving pan with enough water just to cover them. Simmer gently for about 2 hours or until quite tender. Cool. Line a colander with muslin, cheesecloth or loose-woven teatowel and put the apple mush into it. (Or use a jelly bag.) Let the contents drip through overnight. You can give it a slight helping squeeze: most recipes advise that you resist the temptation to squeeze it for fear of making the jelly cloudy, but my experience is that the resulting juice will be cloudy anyway and that it will clear when you add lemon juice.

Measure the juice. To every 1 litre / 1²/₃ pints (US 1 quart) juice, add 700 g / 1 lb 9 oz (US 3¹/₂ cups) sugar. Stir it into the juice, then bring gently to the boil and continue stirring until no more crystals can be heard crunching about. Add several sprigs of the chosen herb, slightly bruised and the vinegar or lemon juice. Raise the heat and allow to boil for about 20 minutes or until setting point is reached (see Windfall Jelly, page 94). Fish out the herb sprigs. Let the jelly cool before stirring in more of the chosen herb sprigs, or finely chopped – if you do this too soon, it will float to the top. Pour into warm dry jars, cover and leave for a month or two to mature.

TOASTED GOAT'S CHEESE WITH SAVORY ON SALAD LEAVES

Fresh goat's cheeses are slid under the grill, set over a dressed salad and sprinkled with savory, whose peppery fragrance is unleashed by the heat of the cheese. Serve with herb bread (page 73).

SERVES 4

4 fresh goat's cheeses: 40-50 g / 1¹/₂-2 oz each
mixed salad leaves: lollo rosso, rocket (US arugula), oakleaf, curly endive, purslane etc
100 ml / 3¹/₂ fl oz oil

2 tbsp white wine or herb vinegar (page 70)
salt and pepper
1 tsp mustard
a pinch sugar
several sprigs savory, leaves only

Put the cheeses on a sheet of foil on a dish or pan which will go under the grill (US broiler). Arrange the salad leaves on 4 plates. Shake together a dressing made from the oil, vinegar, salt, pepper, mustard and sugar and sprinkle it on the salads. Heat the grill to maximum and grill the cheeses until lightly golden and bubbly. Lift them on to the salads and sprinkle savory over the top.

COUSCOUS SALAD

This salad goes particularly well with barbecued lamb.

SERVES 6-8

*200g / 7oz (US 1 cup) medium-
fine couscous (couscous moyen)*
*2 tomatoes, quartered, seeded and
finely chopped*
*5 tbsp finely chopped spring
onions (US scallions)*

*2-4 tbsp each chopped mint and
parsley*
juice 2 lemons
5 tbsp olive oil
salt and pepper

Soak the couscous in cold water to cover for at least half an hour. Swirl the grains around in the water now and then to keep them from sticking together. Drain it through a fine strainer, then shake it out on to a teatowel to dry further. Put it in a large salad bowl with the remaining ingredients, season generously and mix well. Refrigerate until serving.

CHERRY TOMATOES WITH CREAMY LEMON BALM OR MARJORAM DRESSING

Bite-sized tomatoes in a creamy dressing with plenty of herbs. If marjoram, the flowers can be used as a garnish.

SERVES 4

250g / 9oz cherry tomatoes
*2 tbsp finely snipped lemon balm
or marjoram leaves*

creamy dressing (page 6)
optional: some marjoram flowers

Halve the cherry tomatoes and put them cut side down on a round plate. Stir the chopped herbs into the creamy dressing, pour it over the tomatoes and garnish with the flowers.

WILD HERB BREAD

A lovely loaf to go with summer salads, or with cheese.

MAKES 1 LOAF

*300g / 10oz strong white bread
flour (US 2-2½ cups all-
purpose flour)*
*100g / 3½oz (US ¾ cup)
wholewheat flour and
100g / 3½oz (US 1 cup) rye
flour
or use 200g / 7oz (US 1⅔ cups)
wholewheat flour
and omit rye flour*

2 tbsp bran
2 tsp salt
*15g / ½oz fresh yeast or 1 packet
(7g / ¼oz) fast-action dried
yeast (US 1 package rapid-rise
dry yeast)*
*2-3 tbsp finely chopped fresh
herbs of your choice*
300ml / 10floz lukewarm water
2 tbsp olive oil

In the bowl of the electric mixer, or other large mixing bowl, put the flours, bran, salt, yeast and herbs. Add the water and olive oil and work up to a firm, not too sticky dough using the dough hook or your hands. If the dough is dry, add a little more water; or if too wet, add sprinkles of flour if necessary. Knead thoroughly with the mixer (or turn the dough out and knead on a board by hand) until firm and springy. It should clean itself away from the sides of the bowl, and not be unduly sticky to the hands. Leave to rise in the bowl for as long as it takes to double in size – anything from 1 to 2 hours, depending on the temperature. Knock the dough down and flatten it. Roll it up into a large sausage the length of your loaf pan. Oil the pan and put the dough in. Press it down firmly. Leave it to climb to the top of the pan (about a further 30 minutes).

Heat the oven to 220°C / 425°F / Gas 7 and bake the loaf until well risen and golden-green (about 30 minutes). Turn it out onto a rack to cool.

TOMATO, MELON AND CUCUMBER SALAD WITH MINT

A refreshing summer salad of sweet-sour contrasts which makes a good starter. Serve with home-made herb bread (page 73), French bread with herb butter (page 69) or garlic bread.

SERVES 6

1 ripe melon: Ogen or honeydew
1 cucumber
salt
500 g / 1 lb 2 oz tomatoes
plenty of finely chopped mint

150 ml / 5 fl oz oil
3½ tbsp vinegar
salt and pepper
mustard

Peel the melon and the cucumber, remove the seeds and cut into medium-sized chunks. Put them in a colander and sprinkle with salt. Leave to exude some of their juice for at least an hour, then shake them out well and put them in a large salad bowl. Chop the tomatoes in similar-sized pieces and add them with the mint to the salad. Mix together the oil, vinegar, salt, pepper and mustard to a smooth dressing and pour it over. Chill the salad well. Serve in bowls as it is rather liquid – hence the need for bread to mop up the juices.

COURGETTES À LA GRECQUE WITH WILD HERBS

An appealing dish, especially if you can find (or grow) yellow as well as green courgettes.

SERVES 4

250 ml / 8 fl oz water
4 tbsp olive oil
juice 1 lemon, or 2 tbsp wine vinegar
salt and pepper
2 tbsp finely chopped shallot or spring onion (US scallion)
1 clove garlic, mashed
a sprig fennel

plenty of wild marjoram and/or wild thyme leaves and flowers
1 tsp each peppercorns and coriander seeds
1 large tomato, skinned and roughly chopped
500 g / 1 lb 2 oz courgettes (US zucchini), sliced thickly

Put the water, oil, lemon juice or vinegar, salt, pepper, shallot or spring onion, garlic, fennel, chopped marjoram or thyme leaves, spices and tomato in a wide pan. Bring to the boil and simmer for 10 minutes. Drop in the courgettes and cook for 6-8 minutes or until barely tender. Lift them out with a slotted spoon and put in a serving dish. Boil the juices down hard to reduce to 3 or 4 tbsp. Pour over the courgettes and scatter flowers on top. Serve chilled.

WILD MINT
(AND PURPLE LOOSESTRIFE)

BROCHETTES TRICOLORES ON ROSEMARY SKEWERS

Chunks of lamb shoulder, fillet of beef and pork are threaded on skewers made from rosemary prunings, interspersed with peppers, onions and the odd bay leaf.

MAKES 10 BROCHETTES

10 rosemary twigs: about
    30 cm / 12 inches long
400 g / 14 oz boneless shoulder of
    lamb
400 g / 14 oz fillet of beef (US
    beef tenderloin)
400 g / 14 oz pork fillet (US pork
    tenderloin)

150 g / 5 oz smoked bacon, cut
    1 cm / ³/₈ inch thick
1 red sweet pepper: about
    250 g / 9 oz
4 spring onions (US scallions)
10 bayleaves
olive oil

Remove all rosemary spikes from the twigs and whittle the ends to a sharp point. Cut the meat, bacon, pepper and onions in chunks. Thread them alternately on to the skewers, inserting a bayleaf halfway along the brochette. Sprinkle with olive oil and leave to marinate in the fridge. Barbecue, turning regularly, until golden and fragrant. Serve with a salad of flageolets and French beans, or any of the other salads in this chapter.

LEG OF LAMB WITH A WILD HERB CRUST

Just as good cold as hot (perhaps better), the lamb develops a deliciously aromatic crust as it roasts.

SERVES 6

1·2 kg / 2 lb 10 oz leg of lamb
salt and pepper
3 tbsp mixed wild herbs, finely
    chopped: e.g. thyme, rosemary,
    savory, mint, marjoram

1 tbsp mustard
25 g / scant 1 oz (US ¹/₂ cup)
    fresh breadcrumbs
juice ¹/₂ lemon
1 clove garlic, crushed

If possible, have the butcher remove the upper part of the bone from the lamb. Season the meat. Mix or process together the herbs, mustard, breadcrumbs, lemon juice and garlic to a thick paste. Press it firmly into the skin side of the lamb. Leave the meat in the fridge for a few hours or overnight.

Heat the oven to 220°C / 425°F / Gas 7. Roast the meat for 15 minutes to fix and brown the crust; lower the heat to 180°C / 350°F / Gas 4 and roast for a further 30-45 minutes, depending on how you like your lamb done, basting from time to time. Cover with foil if the crust is becoming too brown.

MARJORAM

PURSLANE

PORTULACA OLERACEA

F: Pourpier. G: Portulak. I first acquired a taste for purslane during our time in Mexico. In the markets, moon-faced, broad-beamed Mexican women, their smooth black hair tied back in lustrous plaits, squatted on the pavement. In front of them lay little piles of this sprawling, red-legged succulent plant with rounded shiny green leaves. Also on offer were papery-husked green tomatoes (tomatillos or *tomates verdes*, of the physalis family), fiery green chillies and bundles of fresh coriander (cilantro), all of which (plus diced pork) were combined to make a dish called *verdolagas en verde* – pork with purslane in a green tomato sauce.

Once back in Europe (and pining for purslane) I discovered some seeds, sowed them and lived to regret it. Come the end of summer, the little fruit capsules catapulted their contents – about a billion black seeds – all over my carefully tended vegetable plot. I have never needed to sow it again. For this reason, if you find it growing in the wild, it may be best to leave it there – although it is easily enough uprooted if you do get an infestation.

Purslane seems to have originated in Asia Minor and was used extensively in ancient Egypt as a vegetable, a spice and also for medicinal purposes. It apparently thrived in Elizabethan England and was much appreciated by the British. Gerard, the sixteenth-century

herbalist, recommended it in a salad dressed with oil, salt and vinegar, 'to cool the blood and cause appetite'. John Evelyn, the English diarist and author, recorded its use as a pickle. An esoteric practice was to strew it around the bed as a protection against evil spells; a more practical approach was to chew it in the belief that it would keep the teeth firmly in place.

This plant is something of an acquired taste. When raw it is pleasantly acid and spicy, with a rich, fleshy texture (one of its less flattering names in English is pigweed). Once cooked it becomes gelatinous, like okra, a quality which serves to thicken sauces – just as a *pied de porc* (pig's trotter) does. The best time to pick it is in high summer, before it flowers. The whole plant, leaves and all but the thickest fleshy stems, can be used, especially if the vegetable is to be cooked. Follow the Mexicans' example and combine it particularly with rich ingredients, such as pork in a sauce, where its acidity makes a good counterpoint. Or do as the English and French do and use it in salads, when it's best to concentrate on the fleshy leaves.

In seed catalogues or in garden centres, you may have noticed some beautiful flowering plants called portulaca (or sun plants). These are varieties which have been selectively cultivated for their wonderfully gaudy blooms and should not be eaten.

PURSLANE SALAD WITH AVOCADO AND BACON

Another great summer salad which can be served as a starter or to go with simply grilled white meats or fish.

SERVES 4

4 handfuls purslane leaves: about 200g / 7oz trimmed weight
creamy dressing (page 6)
1 avocado
juice ½ lemon or 1 lime

150g / 5oz streaky bacon, diced small
fresh herbs in season, finely chopped

Prepare the purslane leaves as above. Make a bed of them on a round serving dish and sprinkle with some dressing. Peel the avocado and cut in 8 segments. Arrange them like the spokes of a wheel over the purslane. Sprinkle with lemon or lime juice. Fry the bacon dice without any fat in a heavy-based pan until golden and crusty. Lift them out of the rendered fat with a slotted spoon and scatter them over the salad. Sprinkle on the chopped herbs and serve.

WARM SALAD OF PURSLANE WITH CHICKEN LIVERS AND HERB VINEGAR

All the (considerable) goodness and intriguing flavour of purslane is conserved if it is eaten raw rather than cooked.

SERVES 4

4 good handfuls purslane: about 200g / 7oz trimmed weight
150ml / 5floz oil, of which a proportion can be walnut oil
4 tbsp vinegar
1 tsp coarse grain mustard
1 tsp honey
salt and pepper

350g / 12oz chicken livers, trimmed and chopped
2 tbsp oil
3 tbsp flavoured vinegar: e.g. wild garlic, elderflower page 57, herb page 70 or raspberry page 82

Pull the leaves off the purslane, wash and spin them dry; discard the stalks. Whisk together the oil(s), vinegar, mustard, honey, salt and pepper to make a thick dressing. Arrange the purslane on four plates and sprinkle the dressing on top. Season the chicken livers and fry them in the hot oil for 2-3 minutes until just stiffened but still pink inside. Scatter them over the salads. Deglaze the pan with the vinegar and sprinkle on top. Serve at once.

PURSLANE AND MELON SALAD WITH PRAWNS

A colourful opener to a summer meal with a particularly pleasing clash of textures and flavours: fleshy green purslane, soft melon chunks and sweet prawns.

SERVES 6

3 handfuls purslane: about 150g/5oz trimmed weight
1 pink-fleshed melon
creamy dressing (page 6)

30 peeled cooked prawns (US shrimp)
chopped fresh herbs al gusto

Strip the leaves off the purslane and discard the stalks. Arrange the leaves around the edge of 6 salad plates. Cut the melon in half, discard the seeds and scoop out the flesh with a melon scoop. (Or peel the melon, cut in half, remove seeds and dice fairly small.) Put a heap of melon flesh in the middle of the plate.

Pour some dressing over the purslane and melon. Arrange the prawns on top of the salads and sprinkle with the chosen herbs.

DICED PORK IN A SPICY TOMATO SAUCE WITH PURSLANE

The rich, slightly gelatinous quality of purslane contrasts well with pork in a spicy tomato sauce. Serve with rice.

SERVES 4

500g/1lb 2oz lean boneless pork, diced
salt
2 tbsp oil or lard
500g/1lb 2oz tomatoes, skinned and roughly chopped

2 hot green chillies, seeded and finely chopped
1 clove garlic, mashed
1 onion, finely chopped
200g/7oz purslane with stems, finely chopped

Put the pork pieces in a wide pan with water just to cover and salt. Cover and cook gently for 20 minutes. Raise the heat to evaporate the water. Add 1 tbsp oil or lard to the pan, then stir the meat so that it browns and forms a crust. Remove the meat with a slotted spoon. Blend together the tomato flesh, chillies, garlic and onion in a blender or food processor to a smooth purée. Heat the remaining oil or lard in the pan and throw in the purée, stirring hard. Season with salt to taste. Allow to cook, stirring occasionally, until thick and somewhat reduced (about 10 minutes). Add the purslane to the sauce in the pan along with the meat and simmer for 5-6 minutes more.

PURSLANE AND MELON SALAD WITH PRAWNS

WILD RASPBERRY *RUBUS IDAEUS*

F: Framboise sauvage. G: Waldhimbeere.

WILD STRAWBERRY *FRAGARIA VESCA*

F: Fraise des bois. G: Walderdbeere.

Lucky Linnaeus, who confined himself to a diet of wild strawberries for a time in an attempt to cure his gout. Modern remedies are altogether more banal – and nowadays you would be fortunate to find enough of these precious berries to keep body and soul together for more than an hour or two. Perhaps he had an equal regard for wild raspberries: the Latin name he chose for them means 'berry of Mount Ida', the sacred mountain in Crete where the infant Zeus was said to have grown up, nourished (we may suppose) by the ash-nymphs on scented honey and wild raspberries. Long before Linnaeus, the wild strawberry was one of the fruits dedicated to the Virgin Mary. Study the Madonna in the fifteenth-century painting *La vierge aux buisson de roses* by Martin Schongauer in the Dominican church in Colmar, and from beneath the folds of her rich red robe you will see a perfectly depicted wild strawberry plant bearing both flowers and fruit.

Such impeccable and old-established credentials indicate

WILD RASPBERRY

the high esteem in which both fruits have always been held. Not only the fruit, but also the leaves (and in the case of strawberries, the roots) have been used and valued over the centuries. Crushed wild straw-berries were advocated for maladies as diverse as sun-burn, freckles and discoloured teeth, while the leaves (whose aroma Bacon compared favourably with that of roses) were dried and used both externally (to treat anything from sore throats to painful piles) and internally as a delicious tea. Wild raspberries were bruised to extract maximum flavour and made into a syrup or sweetened vinegar, recommended for feverish conditions and sore throats; and the use of raspberry leaf tea in the later stages of pregnancy has a long history.

Finding wild strawberries is always a race between me and Monsieur Simon, the farmer. It's not so much that he shares my fondness for them (though well he may), more that if I don't keep a sharp eye on things, he has gone down the lane ahead of me with his scythe and given a seasonal 'short-back-and-sides' to the banks where they grow. It's a job to fill even the most modest pot with wild berries. The hunt is on by early June as the sounds and smells of haymaking are in the air. The long grass is parted, crushed salad burnet gives out cucumbery smells and the cows in the field up above munch contentedly on the cud. Soon the strawberries

80

give themselves up, betrayed by their beautiful colour, like little spots of blood in their green and leafy.

Wild raspberries are a lot less vulnerable to passing scythes. The problem is that, coming a little later than wild strawberries when the vegetation is at its most rampant, they tend to disappear beneath the competing jungle of brambles, nettles, mare's tail and other mid-summer greenery. A machete to carve your way through the undergrowth might not be a bad idea, though you might get some funny looks from the neighbours as you set off on your morning walk. In early summer it can be quite difficult to distinguish the wild raspberry plant from the blackberry as their leaves are rather similar. Raspberry stems (the woody ones will bear fruit this year, the green ones next) are smooth and innocuous; the black-berry's are barbed and beastly.

Once the raspberries are ripe, there is no doubt: though the wild fruit is smaller and less plentiful than its cultivated counterpart, what it lacks in size and quantity it more than makes up for in quality. The berries are intensely perfumed, as if conscious that they need to pack ino a small space all the flavour that a bigger berry has more room to spread around. Picking is a labour of love: arms and legs are lacerated and the basket or bowl takes forever to fill. But it's worth it.

WILD STRAWBERRY

A few people sacrifice their wild berries to jam; in some countries the fruit (especially wild raspberries) is made into a spirit, such as the famous *Himbeergeist* from the Black Forest. (In Germany the distinction is made between a *Wasser* and a *Geist*. The former is made from fruit such as cherries and plums which have enough natural sugar of their own to produce the necessary alcohol to preserve the fruits. The latter is produced by long maceration of fruit such as raspberries, blueberries or blackberries, whose sugar content is lower, in a neutral alcohol and then distilling them.) In 1640, John Parkinson wrote of wild strawberries that 'water distilled from the berries is good for the passions of the heart caused by perturbation of the spirits'.

But so fine and fugitive are the flavour and fragrance of both wild strawberry and wild raspberry that it seems to me a tragedy to do much to either of them. At the most, they lend themselves as a garnish to delicately flavoured tarts, creams or ice creams. Or you can add a few wild berries to a salad of (cultivated) summer fruit to enhance the latters' somewhat tamer flavour.

WILD RASPBERRY VINEGAR

Because wild raspberries are so aromatic, only a few are needed to make a well-favoured vinegar, which makes a special present (if you can bear to part with any). *Le choix judicieux d'un vinaigre, c'est ce qui distingue le Cordon Bleu du 'gâte-sauce'* (Guide de l'anti-consommateur, Dorothée Koechlin-Schwartz & Martine Grapas) – or: the correct choice of vinegar is what distinguishes the Cordon Bleu from the sauce-spoiler. A splash of home-made vinegar added to the juices in the pan after searing meat (duck breasts, steak, liver) and a bit of butter gives a short little 'sauce' of character.

MAKES ABOUT 1 LITRE/1⅔ PINTS (US 1 QUART)

2 handfuls wild raspberries: 2-3 tbsp sugar
* about 250g/9oz*
1 litre/1⅔ pints (US 1 quart)
* white wine or cider vinegar*

Put the raspberries in a glass jar with a non-corroding lid, at least 1·5 litres/2⅓ pints (US 1½ quarts) capacity. Pour in the vinegar and add the sugar. Gently shake or stir until the sugar dissolves. Leave on a sunny windowsill for 2-3 weeks, turning from time to time. Strain the vinegar through a colander, then once again through a fine cloth. Bottle up and label.

ELDERFLOWER CRÊPES WITH WILD STRAWBERRIES

If your stocks of wild berries are very meagre, fill the crêpes with cultivated ones and use the few wild ones to scatter over the top. Ice cream and/or elderflower *crème anglaise* (page 58) can be served additionally.

SERVES 4-8

125ml/4floz water juice of 1 orange or 2tbsp
125ml/4floz milk Himbeergeist or eau de
100g/3½oz (US ⅔ cup) flour vie de framboise sauvage
a pinch salt 250ml/8floz single or
3 tbsp sugar whipping cream (US light or
1 tbsp oil or melted butter heavy cream)
2 eggs 3-4 elderflower heads
500g/1lb 2oz strawberries
* and/or raspberries*

Put the water, milk, flour, salt, sugar, oil or melted butter and eggs in a blender or food processor and blend to a smooth batter. Toss the berries with a little sugar and the orange juice or raspberry spirit and leave to macerate.

Just before making up the crêpes, snip the elderflowers into the batter and blend again. Put a film of oil in a non-stick pan 15 cm/6 inches in diameter and wipe it out with absorbent paper. Heat the pan until smoking, then pour in enough batter to film the bottom; pour back any excess into the blender jar. Turn the crêpe once, then turn out on to a plate. Continue with the batter till all is used up.

Fill the warm crêpes with the cool berries, fold them over, pour on some cream and scatter any spare elderflowers and/or berries on top. Serve 1 or 2 per person, depending on your menu.

HONEY CHEESECAKE WITH WILD BERRIES

A light and delicate 'cheesecake' made with *fromage frais*, sweetened with honey and baked in a fragile pastry crust. A small handful of wild strawberries or raspberries (which is about all I ever seem to find) makes a beautiful garnish. If you have enough to cover the whole cheesecake, so much the better.

SERVES 6

200g/7oz shortcrust pastry (US basic piecrust) or puff pastry
400g/14oz fromage frais or Greek yogurt
125g/4½oz (US ⅓ cup) honey
3 eggs, separated
grated zest and juice ½ lemon
2 tbsp sugar
icing sugar (US confectioners' sugar) for sprinkling
wild strawberries or wild raspberries

Roll out the pastry to fit a 26cm/10½ inch quiche tin with a removable base. Chill it while you prepare the filling.

Put a heavy baking sheet into the oven and set the temperature to 180°C/350°F/Gas 4. Process or beat together the *fromage frais* or yogurt, honey, egg yolks, and lemon zest and juice. Whisk the egg whites to a soft snow, add the sugar and continue beating till stiff but not dry. Fold and cut them into the *fromage frais* mixture using a wire whisk. Pour the mixture into the pastry case, place it on the hot baking sheet and bake for about 40 minutes or until golden brown and not unduly wobbly when nudged.

Run a knife around the edge of the pastry and remove the ring of the quiche tin. Slide a palette knife underneath the cheesecake to make sure it hasn't stuck. Place a cooling rack upside down over the cheesecake and invert it onto the rack. Leave it to cool upside down – this prevents the liquid in the *fromage frais* running into the pastry and making it soggy. Once cool, set it right side up again on a good plate, sprinkle with icing sugar and garnish with the berries.

ICED 'SOUP' OF SOFT FRUITS WITH WILD STRAWBERRIES AND RASPBERRY COULIS

Seasonal red fruits are bathed in a sauce of wild strawberries and raspberries, lightly sweetened and given a judicious splash of *Himbeergeist*. Serve in small soup cups or dessert coupes with a sprig of mint and some nice biscuits or cookies to accompany.

SERVES 8

150g/5oz each wild strawberries and raspberries
sugar to taste
2 tbsp Himbeergeist
about 1kg/2¼lb assorted soft fruits: strawberries, raspberries, cherries, black grapes, black- and redcurrants etc

Put the wild strawberries and raspberries in a blender or food processor with sugar to your taste and blend till smooth. Push through a sieve to eliminate raspberry seeds, then stir in the *Himbeergeist* and slacken to a pouring consistency with water.

Prepare all the soft fruits and put in a mixing bowl. Add the fruit coulis and turn the fruit in it to mix well. Chill for several hours or overnight. Garnish with mint sprigs before serving.

FROZEN CHOCOLATE MARQUISE WITH HIMBEERGEIST AND WILD RASPBERRIES

A silky smooth and sinfully rich chocolate 'cake' spiked with raspberry spirit, covered with a layer of Greek yogurt and topped with raspberries. It will taste as good as the chocolate you put into it; the yogurt and raspberries make a delicious contrast.

SERVES 6-8

100 g / 3½ oz petit beurre or
digestive biscuits (US graham
crackers)
50 g / scant 2 oz (US 3½ tbsp)
melted butter
200 g / 7 oz best-quality 'bitter'
chocolate: Lindt excellence,
Terry's Bitter, Nestlé Dessert
etc

3 tbsp water
3 eggs, separated
75 g / 2½ oz (US 5 tbsp) soft
butter
2 tbsp Himbeergeist or eau de
vie de framboise sauvage
a pinch salt
about 150 ml / 5 fl oz Greek yogurt
(wild) raspberries for the top

Put the roughly broken up biscuits in the food processor and process till in fine crumbs. Pour the melted butter through the funnel. Press a layer of buttery crumbs into the bottom of an 18 cm / 7¼ inch springform cake pan. Chill the crumb crust for at least 30 minutes.

Meanwhile, put the chocolate in a heavy-based pan with the water and melt over very gentle heat. Stir until smooth and glossy, then remove it from the heat. Beat together the egg yolks and soft butter until pale and fluffy. Beat in the melted chocolate and the raspberry spirit.

Beat the egg whites with the pinch of salt until soft and snowy. Fold some of the egg whites into the chocolate mixture to loosen it up a little, then scoop all the chocolate mixture into the remaining egg whites and lift and fold the whites into it with a wire whisk until smooth. Pour the mixture into the crumb case and freeze until firm – at least 3 hours, or overnight if you wish.

Just before serving, release the cake from the springform, spread a layer of Greek yogurt on top and garnish with the raspberries.

AUTUMN

BLACKBERRY

RUBUS FRUTICOSUS

F: Mûre. G: Brombeere. To be unaware of blackberries, you would have to be a martian recently arrived from outer space. They appear to grow throughout the entire world, frequently where the gardener would rather they did not. In Mexico at the beginning of the rainy season, the '*zarzamora* (blackberry) lady' would arrive on our doorstep each year with a plastic bucket full of the berries. Sated as we were with mangoes, papayas and watermelon, we fell on them and made them into jams, jellies and ices.

From an apparently lifeless, viciously prickly and thoroughly unimpressive-looking set of twigs, the leaves start to unfold in early spring and a startling spurt of growth begins. By the end of August the plant is a jungle of stems, leaves, prickles and – here it gets interesting – berries. It's best to pick them before the end of September: legend has it that it is unlucky to eat them after October 10 (Michaelmas Day in the old calendar), after which date they are said to have been cursed by the devil. Apparently, when Lucifer was hurled out of hell by St Michael, he unhappily fell into a bramble bush on the said date, and spitefully spat on the berries, making them unpalatable for any who followed. Be that as it may, the fruit is best picked before autumn is too well advanced, certainly before the first frosts, otherwise it is overblown, wet and often mouldy.

Uses for blackberries are many. Traditionally, the juice was prescribed as a mild sedative for those of menopausal age, and a soothing tisane was made from the leaves (fresh or dried) of blackberry, raspberry and woodruff. The old English pie of blackberry and apples is hard to beat, especially if the apples are nicely tart to make up for the slight lack of acidity in the berries. Instead of putting *crème de cassis* (blackcurrant liqueur) in your Kir, try *crème de mûre* (blackberry liqueur) for a piquant alternative. 'Black-berries … can be made into wine that is not so bad as some homemade wines' remarks Euell Gibbons in *Stalking the Wild Asparagus*. Faint praise is so damning.

BLACKBERRY SORBET

Sorbets can be made at home without a fancy ice cream machine, using the food processor to eliminate ice crystals: make a purée sweetened to taste, semi-freeze, then tip into the processor and process with an egg white to a smooth snow.

MAKES ENOUGH FOR 4-6

1 kg / 2¼ lb blackberries
100 g / 3½ oz (US ½ cup) sugar,
*   or to taste*

1 egg white
2 tbsp crème de mûre or de cassis

Put the cleaned blackberries in a heavy pan with the sugar, cover and cook gently for about 5 minutes so that the juice runs. Purée the berries in a blender or food processor, then push through a sieve. Taste the purée and add more sugar if it is not sweet enough to your taste. Tip the mixture into a metal bowl and freeze it until fairly hard around the edges but still a bit soft in the middle. Turn it into the food processor and process until smooth. With the motor running, pour the egg white down the funnel and continue processing until smooth and snowy. Add the liqueur and freeze again.

BLACKBERRY CHARLOTTE MOUSSE CAKE

A lightly set blackberry mousse is encased in Swiss roll-style slices of sponge spread with blackberry jam and moulded in a springform tin. Release it from its corset for serving on a large white or glass plate, and serve some extra blackberries and whipped cream (or Greek yogurt) with it.

SERVES 6-8

3 eggs
200 g / 7 oz (US 1 cup) sugar
100 g / 3½ oz (US ⅔ cup) flour,
*   sifted with a pinch salt*
3-4 tbsp blackberry jelly or jam,
*   or lemon curd*
6 sheets gelatine, or 1 tbsp

powdered unflavoured gelatine
5 tbsp water
500 g / 1 lb 2 oz blackberries
2 tbsp crème de mûre or cassis
500 ml / 16 fl oz whipping cream
*   (US heavy cream)*

Make the sponge sheet: heat the oven to 180°C / 350°F / Gas 4. Prepare a rectangular paper case 30 × 40 cm / 12 × 16 inches from non-stick baking paper (as for a Swiss / jelly roll) and fix the corners with staples. Beat together the eggs and half of the sugar at high speed until thoroughly fluffy and tripled in bulk; the beaters should leave distinct tracks in the mixture. Sprinkle on the flour in several batches and fold it in carefully. Smooth the batter into the paper case and bake in the preheated oven for 10-12 minutes or until barely golden and springy to the touch. Invert the sponge over a teatowel and trim away any ragged edges. Spread it thinly with blackberry jam or jelly or lemon curd and roll it up. Wrap it in foil or cling-film and freeze it, to facilitate slicing later.

For the mousse, soak the gelatine sheets in a bowl of cold water until floppy. Squeeze them out and dissolve gently in the 5 tbsp water. (Alternatively, sprinkle the powdered gelatine on to the 5 tbsp water and let it get spongy, then dissolve it gently.) Cook the blackberries in a covered pan with the remaining sugar until the juice runs – about 6-7 minutes. Cool, then purée until smooth in the food processor or blender. Push through a sieve. Mix in the *crème de mûre* or *cassis* and hot gelatine. Whip the cream into peaks and fold it into the cooled fruit mixture.

Slice the rolled sponge as thinly as you can, and certainly not more than 1 cm / ³⁄₈ inch thick. Arrange the slices around the sides and on the base of a 22 cm / 10½ inch springform cake pan which is at least 6 cm / 2½ inches deep. Pour in the mousse and tap the pan firmly to settle the mixture in. Chill till firm.

To serve, release the springform, lift the charlotte from the base and set on its serving plate. Decorate with some fresh blackberries and leaves (if available) and serve with whipped cream.

BLACKBERRY AND APPLE BOMBES SURPRISES

A recipe which plays on the familiar blackberry and apple theme: a nugget of home-made blackberry ice cream encased in an apple sabayon ice, frozen in yogurt pots for easy unmoulding. Serve with a fruit sauce, made of extra wild blackberries cooked, sweetened and sieved. For a less complicated pudding, serve the blackberry ice cream alone.

MAKES 8

500g / 1 lb 2 oz blackberries
225g / 8 oz (US 1 cup + 2 tbsp)
  sugar
100 ml / 3½ fl oz water
6 egg yolks

500 ml / 16 fl oz whipping cream
  (US heavy cream)
1 whole egg
100 ml / 3½ fl oz apple juice
2 tbsp apple brandy or Calvados

For the blackberry ice cream, cook the blackberries with 50g / scant 2 oz (US ½ cup) sugar until the juice runs – about 5 minutes. Purée in a blender or food processor. Sieve to eliminate seeds.

Make a syrup with the water and 100g / 3½ oz (US ½ cup) sugar: allow the sugar to dissolve first over gentle heat, then turn up the heat and boil to the thread stage. To test, dip a fork into the syrup, blow on it to cool some-what, then pinch a little of it between finger and thumb. A thread should form between the two. If not, prolong the cooking a bit. When thread stage is reached, remove from the heat. Beat 3 of the yolks until well creamed, then pour on the hot syrup in a steady stream and continue beating until the mixture is very pale, thick and mousse-like. Mix this with the fruit purée. Whip the cream to soft peaks. Fold half of it into the fruit mixture and freeze.

Make the apple sabayon: in a large bowl set over a pan of barely simmering water beat together the remaining egg yolks, whole egg, the remaining sugar, the apple juice and liqueur until light, fluffy and tripled in bulk. Allow it to cool a little. Fold the remaining cream into the cooled apple sabayon.

Remove the blackberry ice cream from the freezer and allow it to soften a little. With an ice cream scoop, make 8 nice rounded scoops and put in the bottom of 8 yogurt pots. Cloak with the apple sabayon. Freeze.

To serve, run a knife round the *bombes*, unmould and place them over a blackberry coulis: cook some more blackberries with sugar to taste, sieve and slacken the coulis with a little water. A little *crème de mûre* (blackberry liqueur) could usefully be added for heightened flavour.

BLACKBERRY VINEGAR

Fill a clean dry jar (with close-fitting, non-corroding lid) half full with blackberries. Cover with white wine vinegar and a lid. Turn the berries in the vinegar gently, then leave on a sunny windowsill for several weeks, turning occasionally to mix well. Once the vinegar is a beautiful dark purple, strain it once through a colander into a bowl or jug, and once again through muslin or cheesecloth. Decant into bottles, cork and keep for a month or two before using in salad dressings, to deglaze pans after frying duck breasts or steaks, or for sharpening up sauces for game or other strongly flavoured foods.

CEP

BOLETUS EDULIS

F: Cèpe, bolet. G: Steinpilz, Herrenpilz. When first you pick a cep, you are immediately aware that you have met a serious mushroom. Heft it in your hand: it is unbelievably heavy and dense – one of its names in German means 'stone mushroom'. Another is 'gentleman's mushroom'. Ceps are certainly officer's food, perhaps the finest of all wild mushrooms. Sadly, snails, slugs and maggots share our fondness for it and it is rare to find one which is not shot through with holes, at least in the stem.

The cep belongs to the fairly large *boletus* family. Its brown cap (which can vary in colour from beige to chestnut) is soft and pleasing to the touch; run your finger over it and it feels a bit like chamois leather. Its stem balloons out in a pear-like, almost obese form. It has one distinctive and unmistakable characteristic, common to all the boletus family: instead of gills, like most mushrooms, it has tiny, sponge-like pores. The effect is a bit like the imprint left behind when you pull the choke away from the artichoke heart. The size of this wonderful beast can vary from a few centimetres across the top of the cap to something the size of a sombrero. The smaller ones are best; the large ones make wonderful photographs, but less good eating as their pores are often soft and mushy.

Not all the boletus family are edible, and of those which are, the cep is far and away the most valuable. Less good but still valid is the bay boletus (*B. badius*). (Where we live, the locals seem to refer to *B. edulis* as *cèpes* and *B. badius* as *bolets.*) Like the cep, the bay can grow to an impressive size, but its cap is a darker brown (bay rather than chestnut) and the pores pale yellow to yellowish green, bruising blue when pressed. This blue bruising – though it looks alarming – should not deter you as long as the pores are yellow to green. It's the red pores which are bad news: a good rule, and one which is summed up in an important and easily remembered German jingle (at least for those who

speak German) is:

'Von Pilzen mit roten Röhren
lass dich nicht betören!'

which means (roughly): watch out for any mushroom with red pores. The (in)famous Satan's (or Devil's) boletus (*B. satanas*) is the chief offender, but with its reddish orange stem and blood-red pores, it is quite impossible to mistake it for an edible boletus.

A good place for cep hunting is along the fringes of woods, where they are sometimes to be found sitting up boldly in the wispy grass. Around us, they start to appear in high summer, and go on well into the autumn – I remember being surprised and sceptical that they were indeed ceps when I first found some, having always thought of them as exclusively autumnal. Fresh, they can be sliced and cooked with lots of garlic and parsley: their robust flavour and texture allows some quite assertive combinations.

Because of their pronounced flavour ceps also dry well, a process particularly suited to the larger ones. If the pores are soft and wet, cut or pull them away and use only the caps. Cut in slices, thread them necklace-style and hang to dry in a warm, dark place. Then put them in an airtight container. These mushrooms can be used to perfume culinary oils, or a risotto, or pasta. Smaller, broken pieces can be chopped finely and used as you would a breadcrumb coating, for meat, fish or offal.

DRIED CEPS IN OIL

If you were once the lucky recipient of some dried ceps (or you've just discovered a cache of your own, made in a fit of enthusiasm and then forgotten), here's one idea: place them in a wide-necked jar with lid and fill up the jar with a tasteless salad oil. Cover and leave in a dark place for several months. The ceps will not soften in the oil, so before using them you will need either to soak them in boiling water, or to put them into dishes which have quite a lot of liquid and a fairly long cooking: risotto, or the gratin which follows. The oil will be wonderfully flavoured and will be used selectively to enhance any dish calling for an interesting oil.

CEP-STUFFED QUAILS WITH TOMATO AND MARJORAM SAUCE

The firm flavour (and texture) of ceps makes an excellent foil for the delicate flesh of quails, and you don't need many of them for this filling. *Rösti* (page 62) makes a good accompaniment, and the whole dish looks a picture: roasted birds on a bright red sauce with golden brown *Rösti*.

SERVES 6

3-4 beefsteak tomatoes	*6 quails*
1 medium onion	*1 shallot, finely chopped*
2 cloves garlic, mashed	*200g / 7oz ceps, cleaned and*
2 tbsp olive oil	*finely chopped*
salt and pepper	*200g / 7oz pork or veal sausage,*
a pinch salt	*skinned*
a handful wild marjoram leaves,	*1 egg*
snipped with scissors	

Start by making the tomato sauce. Remove the cores from the tomatoes and chop them roughly. Purée them in food processor or blender with the onion and one clove of garlic until quite smooth. Heat 1 tbsp oil in a heavy pan and throw in the purée. Season with salt, pepper and sugar, add marjoram and simmer for about 25 minutes or until thick and syrupy. Push the sauce through a sieve to eliminate skin and seeds. Set the sauce aside.

Remove the breastbones from the quails: cut down to each side of the breastbone, open up the flesh and cut away the breastbones and rib cage with scissors or shears, leaving a bony base on which to set the stuffing. Season the birds inside and out.

Soften the shallot and the second clove of garlic in some more oil without browning. Add the ceps, cover and cook gently for 5-6 minutes. Uncover the pan, raise the heat and allow the juices to concentrate and evaporate. Put the ceps into a bowl (or the food processor) and add the sausage and the egg. Mix (or process) together roughly. Check the seasoning.

Place about 2 tbsp filling on each of the boned quails. Bring the breast flesh up and over the filling, and join the skin together again with large loopy stitches, using a darning needle and double black thread (easier to see for removal later). The birds can be prepared ahead up to this point and refrigerated until needed.

Sprinkle the birds with a little olive oil. Heat the oven to 220°C / 425°F / Gas 7 and roast them for 18-20 minutes or until golden brown. Remove the threads, cut the quail in half and lay them on a serving dish or heated serving plates face down. Serve with the hot tomato sauce.

RAMEKINS OF CEPS AND SMOKED HAM

Freshly fried garlicky ceps are baked in a savoury custard with smoked ham. Makes an excellent starter; or bake it in a gratin or soufflé dish and serve for supper.

MAKES 8 RAMEKINS, EACH 125ML/4FL OZS

1 shallot, finely chopped
1 clove garlic, mashed
1 tbsp oil
400g/14oz ceps, cleaned and
  sliced
salt and pepper
4 slices smoked or raw ham:
  about 100g/3¹/₂oz

300ml/10floz single cream (US
  light cream)
300ml/10floz chicken stock, or
  water + ¹/₂ chicken stock cube
3 eggs

Soften the shallot and garlic gently in the oil. Add the sliced mushrooms, season to taste and cover. Cook gently for 5 minutes, then uncover and cook briskly for 5-6 minutes more until the juices evaporate. Cool. Cut the ham in thin strips. Mix together half the cream, half the stock and the eggs. Check the seasoning. Lightly oil 8 ramekins. Divide the mushrooms and most of ham strips (leave some for the sauce) equally among the ramekins and pour on the egg mixture. Put the ramekins in a roasting tin filled with water and bring just to the simmer. Bake in a 150°C/300°F/Gas 2 oven for 20-30 minutes or until the custards barely wobble when nudged. If they do, prolong the cooking until they are firm.

Bring to a boil the rest of the cream and stock with salt and pepper to taste. Simmer for 5 minutes. Stir in the remaining ham strips. Turn out the ramekins on to heated plates and pour the sauce around them.

GRATIN OF POTATOES AND CEPS

A rather special potato gratin in which stock replaces the more usual cream, the flavoured oil from the ceps replaces butter, and the ceps give a wonderful fillip to the whole. Excellent with duck, game or red meat.

SERVES 6

30g/1oz dried ceps in oil (page
  90): about 2 good tbsp finely
  chopped
300ml/10floz hot beef stock, or
  water + ¹/₂ beef stock cube

1·2kg/2lb 10oz firm, waxy
  potatoes: e.g. Stella, Nicola etc
2-3 tbsp oil from the ceps
salt and pepper
1 shallot, finely chopped

Put the ceps in a bowl and cover with the hot stock (or add boiling water to the ceps and dissolve the stock cube in it). Leave for about 10 minutes. Peel the potatoes and slice them thinly (the slicing blade on the food processor is ideal). Brush an ovenproof gratin dish with oil. (Cast iron is best as the gratin can be brought to the boil on top of the stove before baking, which speeds up the cooking). Lift the ceps out of the stock. Layer the potatoes, chopped shallot and ceps in the dish, sprinkling with more oil and seasoning with salt and pepper as you go. Moisten with the stock, bring to the boil on top of the stove if possible, then bake at 200°C/400°F/Gas 6 for 35-40 minutes or until all the stock is absorbed and the top golden.

CRAB APPLE

MALUS SYLVESTRIS

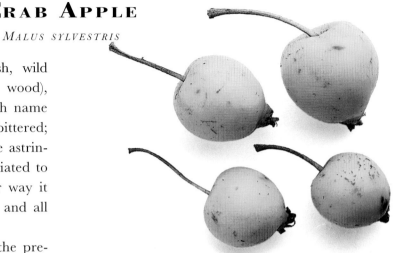

F: Pommier sauvage. G: Holzapfel, Wildapfel. In English, wild apples are crabby, in German woody (*Holz* = wood), and in French just plain wild. From the English name comes the word 'crabby', meaning sour and embittered; or perhaps it was the other way around and the astringent adjective came first, and was later appropriated to describe the flesh of the wild apple. Whichever way it happened, bite into a tiny, wizened crab apple and all will become clear.

The truly wild apple tree (*Malus sylvestris*) – the precursor of our cultivated varieties, for which it is used as grafting stock – seldom grows more than 6 to 8 metres high. When young, its branches are covered in a soft down, and equipped with prickles. However, most apple trees found growing wild are, like cherry trees, orchard escapees which have gone back to nature – *Malus pumila* and others. Whether genuinely wild, or just gone native, the trees grow in hedgerows and on the edges of forests, out in the open where bees can pollinate their beautiful flowers, and where the light will ripen their puny but aromatic little fruits.

In bygone days, crab apple flowers used to be made into fritters; the sour juice of the small, yellowish green fruit was expressed and fermented to make verjuice (*verjus* or 'green juice') and used interchangeably with vinegar (*vin-aigre* or 'sour wine'). Another crab apple delicacy is the so-called crab apple butter (or cheese), made by stewing the apple flesh with sugar (and sometimes cider) to a very thick paste. It is used not only as

a sweet (similar to quince cheese) but also as a relish to serve with cold meats. Where crabs have always come into their own, however, is in jams and jellies for they have an incomparable flavour and plenty of pectin for a good set. They can also serve as the base for flavoured jellies (see herb jelly, page 72), either alone or in conjunction with cultivated apples; or with other wild fruit such as blackberry. Crab apple jelly makes an excellent glaze for open-faced apple tarts, the sort sold by French *pâtissiers* for a small fortune.

Crabs were considered to have medicinal as well as culinary uses. In the old days the cut fruit was applied to warts to dispel them (though incantations were considered to be more effective in hardened cases). The apple was then buried in the garden and as it rotted away (so the theory went) so also the wart disappeared. Verjuice was also held by some to be good for rubbing on sore breasts, which must make it a strong contender (along with rubbing nettles into rheumaticky joints, see nettles, page 18) for the prize of most painful remedy for an already painful condition.

In Alsace, traditionally, crab apples were often distilled – for medicinal purposes, naturally. Even today some small private distillers in the Vosges make an *eau de vie de pomme sauvage*, as do those who still enjoy the right to distil a certain amount of spirits without paying tax (*le droit local*). As this right dies out, local interest in these little wild fruits is dwindling.

There used to be a dear old crab apple tree standing proud from the edge of one of the woods near our village. It served as a landmark for farmers, foresters, huntsmen and the organisers of the annual *marche populaire*. Such was its fame that it may even have featured on local maps; and it was always referred to in the local dialect (*d'r Holzöpfelbäum*) which probably made it contemporary with the oldest members of our village (who speak French only with difficulty, having grown up through two German occupations).

One day it blew down in a gale. At the next meeting of the *Conseil Municipal* it was decided to replant, and a young successor was put in its place. Later we read in the parish magazine that it had been vandalised. It has now been quietly replaced and we are crossing our fingers. Meanwhile I am planning to plant a *Malus* in my garden, a John Downie. Described by Robin Lane Fox (*Better Gardening*) as 'the prince of all crabs for fruit', it should see us over the lean period while the Bettlach *Holzöpfelbäum* is settling in.

WINDFALL JELLY

On my walk this morning I picked up some crab apples, some tiny wild pears and a handful of quinces which had rolled down the bank from a neighbour's garden. From what looked like a most unpromising collection of bruised offerings there came a sparkling jelly of a delicate pale amber. Lovely with fresh bread or toast for tea, or for glazing open-faced fruit tarts.

MAKES 6 SMALL JARS

about 2 kg / 4½ lb mixed windfall fruit: e.g. crab apples, apples, pears, quinces, chopped up

roughly with cores and peel
sugar
juice 1 lemon

Put the trimmed and chopped fruit pieces in a large preserving pan and add water just to cover, but not drown, the fruit. Bring to a boil, then reduce the heat and simmer gently for about 2 hours, or until soft. Stir or mash with a wooden spoon as they cook.

Once soft, tip the fruit and juice into a muslin- or cheesecloth-lined colander suspended over a bowl or pan (or use a jelly bag if you have one). Allow the purée to release its juice overnight. It will look cloudy, but will clear when you boil it up with the sugar and lemon juice.

Measure the juice and pour it into the preserving pan. To every 1 litre / 1⅔ pints (US 1 quart) juice add 700 g / 1 lb 9 oz (US 3½ cups) sugar. Boil hard until setting point is reached. To test, put a saucer in the freezer, then tip a little jelly into it and run your finger through it. It should leave a definite channel which does not run back together again. If not, prolong the cooking a little.

Pot into clean dry jars, cover immediately and label.

ROAST DUCKLING WITH CRAB APPLES

The sharpness of the crabs contrasts well with the rich duck flesh.

SERVES 4

1 duckling
a handful crab apples, quartered
   and cored
salt and pepper
a sprig thyme
250 ml / 8 fl oz chicken stock, or
   water + ½ cube chicken stock
   cube

2-3 tbsp crab apple jelly
optional: 1 tbsp Calvados or
   other apple spirit
25 g / scant 1 oz (US 1½ tbsp)
   butter

Prick the duckling all over with a fork and put the prepared crab apples and the thyme inside. Season it and set it on a rack over a roasting pan in which you have put about a cupful of water.

Heat the oven to 220°C / 425°F / Gas 7. Roast the duckling for 25-30 minutes, basting frequently, until the flesh is just cooked: the juice from the legs when pricked will still run a little pink. Leave it in the turned off oven while you prepare the sauce.

Boil the stock down hard to reduce by half, then add any juices from inside the bird. Stir in the crab apple jelly and Calvados or apple spirit (if using). Remove from the heat and whisk in the enrichment butter. Check the seasoning and serve with the duckling.

APPLE TARTLETS WITH CRAB APPLE GLAZE

Thin discs of puff pastry covered with fanned out apple slices and glazed with crab apple jelly. They look chic and taste great, and can even be prepared ahead, deep-frozen and baked straight from the freezer. Serve with ice cream.

SERVES 6

200 g / 7 oz puff pastry
3 best-quality eating apples: e.g.
   Cox's
juice 1 lemon
sugar

about 25 g / scant 1 oz (US
   1½ tbsp) butter, cut in small
   dots
6 tbsp crab apple or windfall
   jelly

Roll out the puff pastry very thinly and cut from it 6 discs each 12 cm / 5 inches in diameter. Lay them on a sheet of non-stick baking paper on a baking sheet. Peel, core and quarter the apples and cut them in very thin slices. Fan them out on the pastry discs, doming them up a little in the middle. Sprinkle with lemon juice to prevent them discolouring, and sugar to taste. Dot with butter pieces. If not to be baked immediately, open freeze them until hard, then stack them up and freeze them in a rigid container.

Heat the oven to 220°C / 425°F / Gas 7. Bake the tarts for 10-15 minutes or until the pastry is golden and the apples lightly caramelized and tinged with brown. Remove from the oven and brush with warmed crab apple jelly.

FIELD MUSHROOM

AGARICUS CAMPESTRIS

F: Champignon des prés.
G: Wiesenpilz.

Today is September 1st. The sky is a cool, clear blue; the air strikes cold on the cheek. A couple of weeks ago the farmer took his second and final cut of hay. Up on the hillside behind the house the short-cropped tussocks of grass are silvery grey with dew. A green woodpecker rattles with annoyance at my arrival. The autumn crocuses, palest mauve like an Edwardian tea gown, catch the rays of early sunlight which slant through the branches of the old apple trees. In the distance the baker sounds his insistent horn on his daily round. Too bad, the breakfast baguette will have to wait. This is a morning for mushrooms.

There are numerous different types of what are loosely termed 'field mushrooms', all members of the *agaricus* family – forty sorts in Britain alone, for instance. They are probably the easiest to find, bright white blobs in the middle of the fields, and the ones with which most people are familiar, related as they are to the shop mushroom. In the southern part of Alsace where we live, the maize stands tall, oilseed rape waxes and wanes with the subsidies, wheat is a constant, and linseed appears from time to time. But sufficient old meadows always remain, never ploughed up, fertilized only by cow pats and mown only by the munching of brown and white dairy cows. This is the natural habitat of the field mushroom.

Within the large *agaricus* family there are several sorts of edible mushrooms which are of interest. Some are flat with dark brownish-black gills, usually quite large and wide open; others have pink gills and may vary in size from small and tightly closed up (in which case the gills are invisible until you slice the mushroom) to plate-sized (when the pink gills are visible). The wide open ones with the black gills are less highly esteemed round these parts, mainly because they have a high water content and go rather limp when cooked. They make wonderful soup, or – for a breakfast *à l'anglaise* – can be grilled and topped with a poached egg, the whole sitting on toast or a brown bap, with a crisp rasher of bacon beside. The pink-gilled sorts (from which the cultivated variety was bred) can be used in any recipe calling for shop-bought mushrooms. The flavour of either sort, compared to those raised in dark tunnels in sterilised compost, is unmatched.

The only agaricus to be avoided is the Yellow Stainer (*A. xanthodermus*) which grows in the same sort of pastures as edible field mushrooms and is similar in all respects but two: it has telltale yellow stains on the cap, and when bruised or cut it smells like carbolic acid. It won't kill you, but it will make you feel very unwell (*'indigeste'*, as my French field guide puts it).

Though field mushrooms are commonly classified as

an autumnal pleasure, I have found them as early as the first weeks of June. It all depends on the weather, and on the pastures, and the mood of the mushrooms. When mushrooming, take a basket and a knife. Carefully pull up the whole fungus, then cut off the foot and clean away any grass or hay sticking to it. If the stem seems to be shot through with holes, persist up to the cap. If still holey, break the cap in two: it may be writhing with maggots, in which case dispatch it.

When you have picked your fill (it's quite difficult to stop; these are the only wild mushrooms which I have ever found growing in any sort of profusion), bear them off home and sort through them. Separate the larger, black-gilled sorts from the pink-gilled ones – they're best cooked separately because of their very differing water content and colouring. Brush or wipe them clean; wash briefly under running water if you must, but never soak in water. If you can't eat or cook them straight away, put the cleaned mushrooms in a damp teatowel-lined colander, the whole overwrapped in a large plastic bag and refrigerate for up to 2 days. If you must freeze them, better to freeze them cooked. They do not dry well and it would be a pity to pickle them, when their lovely flavour would be drowned.

SOUP OF FIELD MUSHROOMS WITH CREAM AND TARRAGON

The large, flat field mushrooms – especially when they are getting a little blowsy and black beneath – make an incomparable soup. The whipped cream enrichment at the end gives the soup a lovely light consistency and turns it a nice moleskin colour.

SERVES 6

1 onion, chopped
1 clove garlic, mashed
25g / scant 1oz (US 1½ tbsp) butter
500g / 1lb 2oz field mushrooms, sliced
salt and pepper
a few sprigs tarragon

2 level tbsp flour
1·5 litres / 2⅓ pints (US 1½ quarts) chicken stock, or water + 2 chicken stock cubes
250ml / 8floz whipping cream (US heavy cream)
finely chopped tarragon

Soften the onion and garlic gently in the butter. Add the mushrooms, season carefully, cover and cook for 10 minutes until the juices run. Sprinkle on the flour and stir it in well. Add the stock, bring to the boil and simmer for 20 minutes.

Liquidize the soup till smooth and return it to the pan. Whip the cream, then whisk it into the soup. Bring almost back to the boil sprinkle with tarragon and serve at once.

Ravioli of Field Mushrooms with a Leek Sauce

Home-made pasta parcels of mushroom served over a light, creamy leek sauce.

SERVES 6

300g/10oz strong white bread
  flour (US 2-2¹/₂ cups all-
  purpose flour)
1 tsp salt
3 eggs
50g/scant 2oz (US 3¹/₂tbsp)
  butter
1 shallot, finely chopped
1 clove garlic, crushed
500g/1lb 2oz fresh field
  mushrooms, finely chopped

juice ¹/₂ lemon
salt and pepper
500g/1lb 2oz leeks, cleaned
  and sliced
4 tbsp water
100ml/3¹/₂floz single cream
  (US light cream)
2 chicken stock cubes

Make the pasta dough: in a food processor or mixing bowl, mix together the flour and salt. Add the lightly beaten eggs and work up to a firm, smooth dough which does not stick to your hands when kneaded. Add sprinkles of flour if too sticky; or a little oil if too dry and granular. Rest the dough while you make the filling.

Heat half of the butter in a large frying pan and soften the shallot and garlic gently. Add the chopped mushrooms, lemon juice and salt and pepper to taste. Cover and cook for about 10 minutes over gentle heat until the juices are released. Uncover, raise the heat and cook until the juices evaporate. Allow the mixture to cool.

Cut the ball of dough in half. Roll out each half very thinly to the size of a teatowel on a floured board. Place teaspoons of mushroom filling over one sheet. Spray or brush the spaces with water. Place the other rolled out pasta sheet on top and press down to seal between the mounds of mushroom. Cut out circles with a pastry wheel or scone cutter. Leave them on a floured board while you prepare the sauce.

Cook the sliced leeks in the remaining butter and the water with salt and pepper to taste until just soft – about 10 minutes. Liquidize with the cream, push through a sieve and return to the pan. Simmer gently for a few minutes; check the seasoning and consistency. If necessary add a little stock or water to give a light pouring consistency.

Cook the ravioli in a large pan of boiling water with the stock cubes for 4-5 minutes or until *al dente*. (Taste the edge, which is double thickness and takes longer to cook.) Drain and serve over the sauce.

FISH FILLETS WITH FIELD MUSHROOMS AND SORREL SAUCE

It is important to choose small pink-gilled mushrooms for this recipe, otherwise they end up a sorry black mess after cooking. The delicate green of the sorrel sauce contrasts sharply with the mushrooms and the fish.

SERVES 4

1 shallot, finely chopped
25g / scant 1oz (US 1½ tbsp) butter
400g / 14oz mushrooms, sliced
salt and pepper
250ml / 8fl oz single or whipping cream (US light or heavy cream)

4 fillets of fresh white fish: cod, haddock, whiting, turbot, sole etc, each about 200g / 7oz
2 good handfuls tender young sorrel leaves, stripped of the central ribs

Soften the shallot in the butter. Add the mushrooms, season to taste and cover the pan. Allow to cook until the juices run. Uncover the pan, raise the heat and allow the juices to concentrate and evaporate. Stir in 2 tbsp cream.

Season the fish and put in a microwave-safe dish. Cover with microwave film and cook on high until just opaque (anything from 3-6 minutes, depending on type of fish used). Alternatively bake the fish in a 200°C / 400°F / Gas 6 oven for 7-8 minutes, depending on the type and thickness of the fish. Drain any juices into a small pan. Keep the fish warm. Add the cream to the juices in the pan and bring to the boil. Add the sorrel and simmer for 5 minutes. Liquidize to a smooth sauce and season to taste. Return to the pan to bubble up a minute or two.

Reheat the mushrooms. Put the fish on heated plates, pour the sauce over and top with a heap of mushrooms.

DICED VEAL OR PORK WITH FIELD MUSHROOMS

If veal is difficult to find, use tenderloin of pork instead. Serve with *Rösti* (page 139, omitting the juniper berries).

SERVES 6

800g / 1¾ lb fillet of veal or pork fillet / tenderloin, diced small
flour
salt and pepper
25g / scant 1oz (US 1½ tbsp) butter
1 tbsp oil
1 small onion or shallot, finely chopped

200g / 7oz firm field mushrooms, sliced
juice ½ lemon
100ml / 3½ fl oz dry white wine
100ml / 3½ fl oz chicken stock (alternatively use 200ml / 7fl oz stock only)
200ml / 7fl oz whipping cream (US heavy cream)

Put some flour, salt and pepper in a plastic bag. Shake the meat in it until lightly coated in seasoned flour. Toss in a colander over the sink to get rid of excess flour. Fry in small batches (no more than will cover the bottom of the frying pan in each batch) in hot butter and oil on both sides until a light crust forms. Remove the meat to a serving dish as it is done and keep it warm. In the same pan (adding a little more fat if necessary to film the bottom) gently fry the onion or shallot. Add the mushrooms and lemon juice, cover and cook for 5 minutes. Uncover the pan, raise the heat and cook hard to evaporate the juices. Add the white wine (if using) and stock and stir and scrape the pan. Allow the liquid to reduce by about half. Stir in the cream and simmer steadily for 5-6 minutes more. Return the meat to the pan and cook for about 5 minutes more to heat it through. Tip it back into the serving dish and serve at once.

HAZELNUT

CORYLUS AVELLANA

F: Noisette. G: Haselnuss. Hazels have always been regarded as enchanted trees, associated since Celtic times with fire, water, fertility and the warding off of evil spirits. They grow fairly commonly throughout Europe in woods, coppices, hedges and by streams. Their strong but supple branches are sought after, along with those of the willow, by basket makers; my father uses the stouter stems to make beautiful straight thumbsticks as presents for favoured family members and friends. Parts of the root are used in marquetry.

While the countryside is still struggling to emerge from winter, the pollen-rich catkins start to appear (to the delight of bees and beekeepers) on the branches of the leafless hazel. Gradually the leaves unfold and buds appear at the extremities of the branches. From these will develop in late summer the nuts,  which grow inside tufted husks, intimately linked in pairs, triplets and even quadruplets – hence, probably, their fertility connotations. When fully ripe they fall readily from the husk to reveal a shiny brown shell; inside the nutshell there is a small round or oval fruit encased in a brown skin (if some other animal has not got in before you).

The nuts have long been esteemed, both medicinally and in the kitchen. Dioscorides apparently considered that though harmful to the stomach, they were good for coughs. (To this day, a tasty folk remedy for an obstinate cough consists of pounded hazelnuts with honey.) The twelfth-century Benedictine nun and visionary Saint Hildegard prescribed them (rather unexpectedly) as a cure for impotence. The leaves served for infusions, or for poultices to be pressed on to painful parts.

In Britain the nuts are known variously as hazelnuts, cobnuts or filberts. Hazelnut is a generic term; it is also the name used to describe the fruit of the wild hazel. Cultivated hazelnuts are known variously as cobnuts (grown anywhere in England), Kentish cobnuts (native to Kent and Sussex) and filberts (usually imported). John Evelyn, the seventeenth-century English diarist, described filberts as 'a kinder and better sort of hasel-nut, of larger and longer shape and beard'. The name filbert is said to come from the French saint and monastic founder St Philibert, whose feast is on 20 August, the date from which the nuts are said to start ripening. In fact, it's usually wise to wait a little longer, at least until the nuts are beginning to fall to the ground unaided. If you pick them too soon they will shrivel away to nothing inside the shell. To store them, take the advice of the Kentish Cobnuts Association's leaflet: remove the husks but do not shell them, and keep in a plastic bag with a little salt to take up any moisture in the air.

Rich in oils, highly nutritious and more digestible than the walnut, the hazelnut can be ground to extract an expensive and wonderful oil. It should never be heated, but used sparingly in vinaigrettes or drizzled parsimoniously over hot vegetables. In parts of rural France where nuts are plentiful there are still fully functioning mills where hazelnuts and walnuts are ground for their oil.

To coax the best nutty flavours out of whole shelled hazelnuts, you can roast them: put them in a shallow baking pan or metal plate and roast dry in a 180°C/350°F/Gas 4 oven until golden and fragrant. Shake the pan a couple of times to ensure even browning. There will be tempting smells of roasted nuts and under the brown husk (rub  one in a teatowel to see) the flesh should be pale golden. The length of time needed varies a lot depending on how fresh (and therefore moist) the nuts are. When ready, let them cool a little, then rub away as much of the brown papery husks with your fingers as you can. Use the nuts whole or broken up and tossed over salads or vegetables; or grind them and use them in sauces and cakes. 'For persons whose teeth are defective, nuts may be ground in a small nut-mill, as made for the purpose' (W. T. Fernie). Or – with care, using the pulse button – grind in the food processor. Don't overdo it, or you will heat them and turn them to a paste.

The Spaniards notably make extensive and original use of hazelnuts in sauces for both meat and fish dishes, a tradition they took with them (along with the nuts) to Mexico at the time of the Conquest. The most famous Spanish sauce is probably *salsa romesco* (or *romescu* – its etymology is about as fiercely disputed as its component parts), a most savoury combination of sweet peppers, tomatoes, garlic, bread, olive oil and roasted and ground hazelnuts. It often accompanies grilled meat or fish, or gets a brief communal simmer with a fish and seafood stew.

Outside the Iberian sphere of influence, hazelnuts are most often used in desserts, particularly in Switzerland, Germany and points east. Swiss pastry cooks and housewives have a delicious habit of putting a layer of ground nuts in the bottom of a pastry case for a fruit tart to serve as waterproofing, as well as giving flavour and crunch. Central European cakes make extensive use of hazelnuts, often to the exclusion of flour: George Lang, in *The Cuisine of Hungary*, points out that Hungarian housewives and pastry cooks consider that to add flour to a nut cake is an abberation.

FRENCH BEAN AND APPLE SALAD WITH TOASTED HAZELNUTS

A salad of good contrasts: beans *al dente* with apple chunks and crunchy toasted hazelnuts.

SERVES 4

300g / 10oz French beans or
    other thin green beans,
    trimmed
1-2 tart eating apples such as
    Cox's, cored and chopped
5 tbsp salad oil
2 tbsp hazelnut oil

2 tbsp cider vinegar
a pinch sugar
salt and pepper
1 tsp coarse grain mustard
50g / scant 2oz (US ⅓-½ cup)
    hazelnuts, toasted (page 101)

Cook the beans in boiling salted water for 10 minutes. Drain and refresh in cold water to set the colour. Put in a serving dish with the chopped apple(s) and a dressing made with the oils, vinegar, sugar and seasoning. Process (using the pulse button of the food processor) or roughly chop the hazelnuts with a little salt and scatter them on top of the salad.

FRENCH BEAN AND APPLE SALAD
WITH TOASTED HAZELNUTS

GUINEA FOWL (OR CHICKEN) WITH A HAZELNUT SAUCE

Pieces of poultry are browned and simmered in stock, and a wondrously rich sauce made by adding roasted ground hazelnuts and *crème fraîche* to the reduced cooking juices. Serve with a green vegetable and some tagliatelle.

SERVES 4

1 guinea fowl or chicken: about
    1·2 kg / 2 lb 10 oz
1 carrot
1 onion
1 stalk celery
1 tsp peppercorns
a bouquet garni
salt and pepper
flour

25g / scant 1oz (US 1½ tbsp)
    butter
1 tsp oil
150g / 5oz (US 1½ cups)
    roasted, ground hazelnuts
    (page 101)
125ml / 4floz crème fraîche, or
    double cream (US heavy
    cream) + juice ½ lemon

Cut the guinea fowl or chicken into 5 pieces (2 legs, 2 wings-with-a-bit-of-breast, 1 breast). Put any other bits of carcass in a pan with the carrot, onion, celery, peppercorns, bouquet garni and water just to cover. Cover and simmer for an hour. Strain the stock and set it aside.

Toss the poultry pieces in seasoned flour. Heat the butter and oil in a wide pan which will take all the pieces in one layer and brown them very briefly on both sides. Add the stock, cover and simmer for 20 minutes. Lift the pieces out and remove the skin; keep warm. Reduce the stock by fast boiling to about a cupful. Stir in the hazelnuts and the cream (and lemon juice if used), check the seasoning and simmer gently for 10 minutes more. Return the poultry pieces to the pan and give them a further 5 minutes' cooking.

BENITA'S HAZELNUT CAKE

A recipe from northern Germany, from one of the best cake bakers I know. Because the cake has no flour it sinks rather after baking, though what it lacks in height it makes up for in damp nuttiness. Like all nut-based cakes, it keeps well. You can also add some grated dark chocolate to the nuts, or make a dark chocolate icing to go on top.

MAKES A 22 OR 24CM/9 OR 10 INCH CAKE

4 eggs
125g/4¹/₂oz (US ¹/₂ cup + 2 tbsp) sugar
125g/4¹/₂oz (US 1²/₃ cups) ground hazelnuts
optional: up to 50g/scant 2oz grated dark chocolate

3 egg whites
a pinch salt
icing sugar (US confectioners' sugar)

Heat the oven to 180°C/350°F/Gas 4. Line a 22 or 24cm/9 or 10 inch springform cake pan with non-stick paper; butter and flour the sides.

Beat together one whole egg with three yolks and the sugar. Then fold in hazelnuts (and chocolate if used). Beat the 6 egg whites with salt until stiff but still creamy, not hard and granular. Fold them in also. Pour into the prepared pan. Bake in the preheated oven for 35-40 minutes or until just firm and a beautiful nut brown; a skewer inserted in the middle should come out clean.

Unmould and cool on a rack – the cake will subside with rather a thump, which is quite normal. When cool, dust with icing sugar and decorate with frosted rose petals or a few toasted hazelnuts.

(If wished, the nuts for the cake can be roasted in the oven (page 101) and ground, for extra nutty flavour.)

HAZELNUT TUILE BOATS WITH CHOCOLATE ICE CREAM

Shaved hazelnuts are sprinkled over a brandysnap/tuile mixture (butter, honey, sugar and flour), baked briefly and draped over a rolling pin to harden. Keep the tuiles in an airtight container until needed and fill with a dark chocolate ice cream.

SERVES 8

50g/2oz (US 3¹/₂tbsp) butter
50g/2oz (US 2¹/₂tbsp) runny honey
50g/2oz (US ¹/₄ cup) sugar
50g/2oz (US ¹/₃ cup) flour, sifted

25g/1oz (US 3 tbsp) shelled hazelnuts, shaved
chocolate ice cream to serve

Melt together the butter, honey and sugar. Remove from the heat and stir in the sifted flour. Mix gently until smooth. Let the mixture cool.

Heat the oven to 180°C/350°F/Gas 4.

Put 16 blobs of the mixture well spaced out on two baking sheets lined with non-stick baking paper. Spread them out very thinly with the back of a wet spoon. They should be no more than 2mm/less than ¹/₈ inch thick. Sprinkle the nuts on top and bake for 5-6 minutes or until pale golden and bubbly. Remove the tuiles from the oven and let them rest for a minute. Then lift them with a palette knife and drape them over a rolling pin. Continue with the rest of the mixture in the same way. When cool, the curved tuiles should be stored in an airtight tin and will keep fresh for a day or two. Fill with chocolate ice cream just before serving.

MISCELLANEOUS MUSHROOMS

What is a mushroom, and what is a toadstool? The distinction – an exclusively English one – is problematic. In Britain, the term 'mushroom' indicates the bought sort: either the button variety, or larger, flattish and black beneath. Just conceivably it might be extended to mean field mushrooms which grow in pastures (page 96). All the rest are designated 'toadstools', and if they grow anywhere near a tree they are doubly suspect. Images of lurid red specimens with white spots float before the eyes, remembered illustrations conjured up from a child's fairytale. Wicked witches with bony fingers lurk in the background. Poison is in the air. In one fell swoop, anything which doesn't come in a plastic-wrapped package is (mentally, if not actually) consigned to the bin.

So where does that leave all those delicious edible mushrooms like ceps, chanterelles and morels, not to mention the host of lesser but no less delicious edible fungi, all of which grow under or near trees? The first types, thrilling to find (because rare), outstandingly good to eat, and fiendishly expensive to buy, each merit a chapter of their own in the book. In addition, this chapter deals with other edible fungi, the sort which in German are loosely and helpfully grouped together as *Mischpilze* – mushrooms to be mixed in with other good things, or indeed other mushrooms. Though some find their way into shops and markets, most will only ever be found, in a nicely jumbled assortment and accompanied by little pieces of moss and twig, in the collector's basket. They are well worth collecting – indeed they will be welcome finds to swell an otherwise meagre catch. For if you are thinking that on your first foray you are going to find armfuls of ceps or morels by the ton, remember Murphy's law for mushroomers: with the exception of field mushrooms, if there's lots of it, it's probably not worth having. In the mushroom hunt, the chase is much more than half the fun. And one year is never the same as another.

There are other miscellaneous mushrooms besides the ones mentioned here which I have not covered for various reasons. These include the ink caps (*Coprinus comatus* and *C. atromentarius*) with which it is considered unwise to drink alcohol. This limits their use in our household. I am not confident of being able to distinguish the fairy ring mushroom (*Marasmium oreades*) from other unsuitable small mushrooms which grow in rings, and most especially from *Clitocybe rivulosa* which is instant death, so I leave them alone. Of the two parasols (*Lepiota procera* and *L. rhacodes*), the first is supposed to be brilliant, and the second to cause gastric upsets. I don't find it easy to tell the difference, and I am influenced by the locals who scorn them. And the giant puffballs (*Langermannia gigantea*) have passed me by – maybe they don't like our soil.

Reluctantly, I have had to omit what we have come to call 'Guy's Grifola'. Guy is my mushrooming neighbour and adviser. Every year at the same time he produces – with a grin and a flourish – a greyish brown monster mushroom which looks a bit like an elderly cauliflower. A hunt through the pages of Roger Phillips' mushroom book reveals it to be a *Grifola umbellata*, that its habitat is 'on the ground arising from a subterranean sclerotium associated with roots of deciduous trees, especially oak', that it is 'very rare', and 'edible'. Guy is certainly not letting on about where his subterranean sclerotium is to be found – and there are plenty of oak trees around here so that's not much of a clue. We are content that each year he returns with another specimen. We break it into florets as he instructs and stew them in butter, garlic and white wine. Wonderful.

The skills required for finding wild mushrooms are similar to those required for playing Pelmanism: you need a prodigious memory for where they turned up the last time you picked them, great persistence, a certain amount of luck and a nose for it. Once you have found them, pull them gently from the ground, with the base intact. (This could be important for identifying purposes when you get back to your books, or to the *Pilzmeister* or the *pharmacie*, and will not affect the mushroom's reproductive ability.) When you are satisfied

they are what you think they are, trim the feet, then brush off any bits of vegetation clinging to them. Either wipe them clean or, in extremis, brush them off briefly under running water. They can be cooked up into little ragouts, pilaffs, risotti or egg dishes. Or they can be pickled in spiced vinegar and used as you would chutney.

Many of them dry well (see individual mushrooms), but for this you must certainly not wash them. Depending on size, leave them whole or cut in slices. Suspend them on a thread, like beads on a necklace, spread out a little so that they do not touch one another. Leave them to dry in a warm, dark place. In Swiss households in the old days, they were spread out on top of the tiled stove to dry, which must have perfumed the *Stube* beautifully. Nowadays you can buy a multi-layered drying apparatus, a bit like a Chinese steamer or a couscoussier. Once dried, the fungi should be stored in a screwtop jar and kept in the dark. This way they keep for months. Soak them in warm water and use as fresh. Alternatively the dried fungi can be ground roughly and used like breadcrumbs for rolling around pieces of meat or game; or finely pulverised for adding to sauces. for grinding use either a pestle and mortar, or the food processor. Don't use the coffee grinder unless you like coffee-flavoured mushrooms.

The **Hedgehog fungus** (*Hydnum repandum*, Pied-de-mouton, Semmelpilz, Stoppelpilz) is a curious beast. Its wavy-edged cap is anything from beige to deep yellow, almost the colour of a chanterelle (page 00). Its paler underside is what gives it away and makes it impossible to confuse with other wild mushrooms: instead of gills or pores, it has little spines – hence its familiar name in English. Jane Grigson in *The Mushroom Feast* calls them rubber brushes, or pig's trotters. In German, *Stoppel* means bristles, which makes sense, though why the French should liken the mushroom to sheep's feet is anybody's guess. It favours the same habitat as chanterelles but is also happy growing on grassy banks or on roadsides. I particularly enjoy finding it because it is usually well concealed, often in tufts of grass or nestling in dead leaves, sometimes in rings. Its flavour is robust and its texture firm and meaty, for which reasons it will stand rather longer cooking than most wild mushrooms. It also dries well.

A relative of *Hydnum repandum* is *H. imbricatum*, a favourite of Swiss mountain mushroomers. In the Valais it is known as *aile d'épervier*: the surface of its cap is scaly and brown, slightly resembling the speckled feathers of a buzzard's wing (hence the name) and the underside bears the telltale *Hydnum* bristles. Very strongly flavoured, the mushrooms are never used fresh, but either pickled and served with raclette or cold meats, or dried, crushed and used as a seasoning, especially with game (another name for it in German is *Rehpilz*, venison mushroom).

HEDGEHOG FUNGUS

HORN OF PLENTY

The **Horn of Plenty** (*Craterellus cornucopioides*, Trompette de (la) mort, Herbsttrompete) is a delicious mushroom whose somewhat grisly French name ('death trumpet') has everything to do with its slightly alarming colour (black) and nothing to do with any ill effects, of which it has none. Horns of Plenty are the last of the wild wood mushrooms to appear, going on well into November if you are lucky. The cornucopia part of their name aptly describes their horn-like shape. The stem, which is hollow, has a pale grey bloom on the outside of it. Don't pick these mushrooms after the first frosts: almost any fungus of whatever colour is blackened by sub-zero temperatures and you may be picking

something which you shouldn't.

Sniff a Horn of Plenty when fresh and you will likely be disappointed. Their excellent, sweetish perfume and flavour seems to develop only when they are dried. A small handful perfumes a risotto or a terrine beautifully. Their earthy flavour seems to go especially well with chestnuts: toss them in butter and add them to a dish of the braised nuts.

A relation of the Horn of Plenty is the Yellow Legs or *Cantharellus infundibuliformis*, similar to look at but with bright yellow legs. It appears in our local supermarket in the autumn, modestly priced and very tasty.

The **Saffron Milk Cap** (*Lactarius deliciosus*, Lactaire délicieux, Edelreizker) is a dramatic-looking mushroom with a cap and stem of brilliant orange, the surface sometimes ringed with concentric circles of darker orange, or even splotched with alarming blue bruises. Break a piece off the cap and droplets of milk the colour of saffron threads will be liberally released. All those members of the (large) lactarius family which when cut or broken weep bright reddish-orange tears are edible. All lactarius which weep white droplets are inedible; some are poisonous. In the Midi, there is a type of lactarius (*L. sanguineus*) whose juice is blood red, somewhat oddly referred to as *le sang du Christ* (the blood of Christ). Down there they are known familiarly as *pinens* or *pinets* because of their habit of growing beneath pine trees. They may be found in coniferous woods, or in fields or gardens beneath pine trees; without conifers you won't find saffron milk caps.

In areas rich in wild mushrooms, they are often scorned. I find them interesting and useful mainly for their wonderful colour and slight crunchiness. As far as flavour is concerned, the 'delicious' part of their Latin name is considered to be something of an oversell. I like to blanch them and mix them with other wild mushrooms, or with game or other highly flavoured meats in sauce. Madame Archimbaud of Serviers, tells me that she uses them in a boeuf bourguignon to replace cultivated mushrooms to excellent effect.

SLIPPERY JACK

Slippery Jack (*Suillus luteus*, Nonette voilée, cèpe jaune, Butterröhrling, Butterpilz) is a fairly common wild mushroom with a glistening (slimy) chestnut-coloured hat and pale gold stem with a ring which looks as though it is in the process of unpeeling, like a banana skin. (The French are more reverential and liken it to a young nun's wimple.) Like the saffron milk cap, it grows beneath conifers. All are agreed that it is edible, though opinions (as often is the case for minor mushrooms) vary sharply on how good it is. The fact that it used to be classed as a boletus, of the cep family (its underside has the same spongy appearance), no doubt boosted its image considerably. One of my German mushroom books calls it a *guter ergiebiger Speisepilz*, faint praise meaning a useful little edible mushroom, while a French guide describes it as *comestible excellent* – the top mark awarded. I find it good but not thrilling. The cap and the ring on the stem (the 'nun's wimple') must be peeled away before cooking. Use in combination with or as a substitute for any of the above mushrooms. Because of its high water content and slight flavour, it does not dry well.

SAFFRON MILK CAP

PASTA WITH 'HEDGEHOGS', SALAMI AND TOMATO

Toss up some 'hedgehogs' with beefsteak tomatoes, garlic and finely chopped *saucissons secs* or salami and serve with spaghetti or tagliatelle.

SERVES 2

FOR SUPPER

1 clove garlic
1 tbsp olive oil
300 g / 10 oz hedgehog fungus, cleaned and sliced
salt and pepper
100 g / 3¹/₂ oz salami, skinned and cut in small cubes
1 large (beefsteak) tomato: about 250 g / 9 oz, skinned and chopped

finely chopped marjoram
2 tbsp single cream or top of the milk (US light cream or half-and-half)
100 g / 3¹/₂ oz spaghetti or thin tagliatelle
grated Parmesan or fromage frais

Soften the garlic in the oil over gentle heat. Add the mushrooms, season to taste and cook gently for 5 minutes. Add the salami, raise the heat and cook to drive off extra juice. Stir in the tomato flesh and cook to a nice, syrupy consistency. Stir in the herbs and the cream.

Cook the spaghetti until just tender. Serve in soup bowls with the mushroom mixture over the pasta and grated Parmesan or *fromage frais* on top.

RAGOUT OF ASSORTED WILD MUSHROOMS

The fruits of a mushrooming expedition in the forest are often fairly meagre – a couple of ceps maybe, a handful of hedgehog fungus, some chanterelles, complemented by rather more field mushrooms gleaned on your way home through the fields. Make them into a ragout, to serve either on its own as a starter, or with grilled white meats. Or you can stir in a little chopped ham and serve the dish for supper.

SERVES 2

1 shallot, finely chopped
1 clove garlic, mashed
1 tbsp oil
350 g / 12 oz assorted wild mushrooms: ceps, hedgehog fungus, chanterelles, field

mushrooms, horns of plenty etc, trimmed and sliced
salt and pepper
squeeze lemon juice
tarragon and marjoram

Soften the shallot and garlic gently in the oil. Add the prepared mushrooms, salt, pepper and lemon juice, cover and cook gently for 5-6 minutes. Uncover, raise the heat and cook hard to evaporate and concentrate the juices. Stir in the chopped herbs and serve at once.

RING OF RICE WITH WILD MUSHROOMS

This dish goes well with kidneys, or calf's liver in a good sauce. It can be cooked ahead of time, pressed into a ring mould and reheated in a bain-marie for serving.

SERVES 4

1 shallot, finely chopped
1 clove garlic, mashed
1 tbsp oil
200g / 7oz mixed wild mushrooms, cleaned and sliced
300g / 10oz (US 1¾ cups) long grain rice

100ml / 3½ floz dry white wine
400-500ml / 14-16floz chicken stock, or water + a chicken stock cube
salt and pepper
butter

Soften the shallot and garlic gently in the oil. Add the mushrooms to the pan, cover and let them cook gently for 5 minutes. Uncover, raise the heat and allow the juices to evaporate. Stir in the rice and toss over moderate heat for about 5 minutes. add the wine and cook till evaporated. Add most of the stock (reserve some; it is hard to judge how much you will need, as the mushrooms vary in their moisture content). Season to taste, cover and cook gently for about 20 minutes. Lift the lid: the rice should have developed holes all over the surface and the stock should have all but disappeared. Taste the rice: it should be *al dente*. If most of the stock is absorbed but the rice still not cooked, add more and continue cooking until it is done. Serve at once. Or, for later reheating, tip the rice into a buttered ring mould (or individual ramekins or dariole moulds). Press it down well. Cover with foil. Reheat in a bain-marie in a 180°C / 350°F / Gas 4 oven for 20 minutes or until thoroughly hot. Turn out to serve.

SAFFRON MILK CAPS WITH BACON, WALNUTS AND CREAM

At just the time that saffron milk caps appear in the woods around us, so also the walnuts start to thud to the ground. Put the two together in this colourful dish, good for supper with polenta or pasta, or small potatoes boiled in their skins. Serve also a sharply dressed salad.

SERVES 3

a 200g / 7oz piece rindless smoked streaky bacon (US slab bacon), sliced thinly across the grain
1 small onion or shallot, finely chopped

300g / 10oz saffron milk caps, sliced and blanched
salt and pepper
12 walnut halves
a little fresh marjoram, chopped
6tbsp sour cream or crème fraîche

Put the slices of bacon in a heavy frying pan without any extra fat. Cook over moderate heat until the fat runs and the bacon is golden and crusty. Discard all but 1 tbsp fat. Add the onion or shallot and allow to soften. Add the blanched mushrooms and season to taste – go easy on the salt, having regard to the saltiness of the bacon. Fry the mushrooms briskly for 5-6 minutes. Stir in the walnuts, herbs and cream, bubble up and serve.

WILD ROSE, DOG ROSE

ROSA CANINA

F: Églantier, cynorrhodon. G: Hagebutte. 'Dog rose' seems an unkind name for so lovely a plant, which graces the hedgerows with its shell pink or white flowers in summer, and lights up with red hips in autumn. Its fruit has long been appreciated as a delicious product of nature, with valuable healing properties to boot: Gerard in his famous herbal commented that rosehips 'when ripe, maketh the most pleasant meats, and banketting dishes as tarts and such-like, the concoction whereof I commit to the cunning cook, and teeth to eat them in the rich man's mouth'.

A great deal of culinary cunning is indeed necessary to make them palatable. And anyone eating rosehips should be equipped not so much with a fine set of teeth as with a very fine hair sieve: the seeds are highly irritant and can have a disastrous effect on the intestines – hence the inelegant alternative French name: *gratte-cul*. The same irritant effect has always endeared them to the school bully, who found a use for them as itching powder and posted them down the necks of unwary classmates.

While dog rose petals (like all rose petals) are edible and can be used to decorate salads and cakes (arrange some over the honey cheesecake on page 83 for a beautiful effect), it is the hips which are most highly sought after. They are nightmarish to pick as the bush is armed with barbed thorns which seem to snag indiscriminately at flesh and clothing and cause untold damage to both. But it's worth it for the jellies or jams they make. They contain abundant vitamin C (four times as much as oranges, claims Richard Mabey in *Food for Free*), a fact which made their harvest extremely valuable in wartime Britain when imported citrus fruits were in short supply. A cottage (or classroom) industry was set up and volunteers enlisted to gather the hips for processing into syrup and jam. As recently as 1964, schoolchildren were still being paid to fetch them.

The vitamin C in rosehips remains even after cooking, though if you value their fresh flavour, try using a quick-cooking preserving sugar (with added pectin) for a quicker set and maximum flavour. The juice is also esteemed in our area, sold pasteurised all year round, and the purée is available in cans to avoid tedious preparation of the hips and the arduous sieving necessary to remove seeds. One way to get around it is to use the sieving disc of the electric mixer, if you have one.

Pick hips after the first frosts: like sloes (page 154) their flavour is improved and they are somewhat softened. (Like sloes too, they are reputed to make an excellent liqueur along the same lines as sloe gin, page 155.) They must be thoroughly washed, topped and tailed, cut in half and the seeds removed. The shells are then cooked, and sieved to remove any traces of the offending seeds and hairs. From the resulting purée jams, jellies and pie fillings can be made. Rosehip jam, something of a tradition in Alsace, is sometimes served with *tarte au fromage blanc*, a classic dessert (similar to the honey cheesecake on page 83 but with sugar instead of honey).

And if you can't face the (admittedly considerable) bother of preparing them for culinary purposes, you can bind them into Christmas wreaths with other seasonal greenery to immense decorative effect.

ALICE'S ROSEHIP JAM

Alice is an old friend who grew up in canton Thurgau in Switzerland, near Lake Constance. Each year she goes to a secret spot near our local hospital to pick a cache of fat rosehips for making into jam, some of which finds its way to the Church bazaar, some into the kitchens of her lucky friends.

MAKES 8-9 JARS

2 kg / 4½ lb fat rosehips   *juice 1 lemon*
sugar, preferably preserving sugar
*   with added pectin*

Wash the hips well, top and tail them and cut them in half. Scrape out the seeds as best you can (Alice uses a melon baller) and put these in a pan with cold water to cover. Put the halved shells in another pan with water to cover. Simmer both pans for 10 minutes, just long enough for the shells to soften. Purée the shells until smooth, then push them through a sieve, using the strained juice from the seeds to aid this process.

Measure the purée: for every kilo you need 750 g–1 kg / 1 lb 10 oz–2 lb 3 oz (US 3¾–4 cups) sugar, depending on how sweet you like the jam. Put the purée in a large wide pan with the sugar and lemon juice. Boil until setting point is reached (the length of time will depend on whether you use pectin-rich sugar or not). Pot up in hot jars, cover when hot and label.

APPLE, SLOE AND ROSEHIP JELLY

A beautifully coloured apple-based jelly which is given a delicious
boost by the sloes and the hips.

MAKES 3-4 JARS

1 kg / 2¼ lb apples
200 g / 7 oz sloes
200 g / 7 oz rosehips

sugar (see method)
juice 1 lemon

Chop up the apples roughly; prick the sloes with a pin all over; top and tail the hips. Put all the fruit in a pan with 2-2.5 litres/3½-4½ pints water. Simmer gently for about 1 hour or until the hips are tender. Turn the contents of the pan into a jelly bag and allow it to drip through for several hours or overnight.

Measure the juice. For every 500 ml / 16 fl oz add 350 g/ 12 oz (US 1¾ cups) sugar. Put in a preserving pan with the lemon juice and dissolve the sugar over gentle heat. Raise the heat and boil hard till setting point is reached (see herb jelly, page 74).

GAME BIRDS WITH ROSEHIP SAUCE

Grouse, partridge or pigeon can be used for this recipe, roasted and a sauce made from the juices, red wine and a little apple, sloe and rosehip jelly (page 114).

SERVES 6

6 game birds
salt and pepper
1 tbsp oil
250 ml / 8 fl oz red wine

250 ml / 8 fl oz chicken stock, or
 water + ½ chicken stock cube
2 tbsp apple, sloe and rosehip
 jelly, or use redcurrant jelly

Season the birds inside and out and brush with oil. Roast them in a 200°C / 400°F / Gas 6 oven for 15-25 minutes, depending on their size and on whether you like them a little pink. Remove them from the oven and keep them warm.

Degrease the pan, add the red wine to the juices remaining and boil hard to reduce by half. Add the stock and reduce again. Remove from the heat and whisk in the jelly. Serve in a little jug to accompany the birds.

HONEY PARFAITS WITH ROSEHIP COULIS

A soft ice flavoured with honey is served over a sharp sauce made with rosehip jam, thinned out with a little juice. The same sauce could be used to accompany vanilla ice cream or the honey cheesecake on page 83.

SERVES 6

3 egg yolks
1 whole egg
175 g / 6 oz (US ½ cup) runny
 honey
300 ml / 10 fl oz whipping or
 double cream (US heavy
 cream)

4 tbsp rosehip jam
juice 1 orange

Beat together the yolks, egg and honey until fluffy and pale and tripled in bulk. Whip the cream to soft peaks and fold it in. Divide the mixture among 6 ramekins or 125 ml / 4 fl oz yogurt pots and freeze.

Slacken the rosehip jam with the orange juice and spoon on to 6 plates, spreading it out with the back of the spoon. Run a knife round the edge of the honey parfaits and turn them out over the sauce. Garnish with a sprig of something seasonal.

WALNUT

JUGLANS REGIA

F: Noix. G: Baumnuss, Walnuss. It is the Year of the Walnut in Alsace. My neighbour Pierrot and his wife Paulette are to be seen daily circling beneath the branches of their two majestic walnut trees in the field just across from my herb garden. Bucket in hand, they stoop frequently to gather the enormous fruit, as big as hen's eggs in a good year. In the evening I can hear the woodpecker patiently hacking away at the ones they missed, for his winter protein stocks. Soon the walnut yields its contents and he flies away. A red squirrel sneaks up, glances furtively at the tree, then scampers up the trunk in pursuit of his own winter booty.

The walnut has long been esteemed as the king of nuts, as demonstrated by its Latin name which could be translated as 'Jove's (or Jupiter's) royal acorn'. It was a favourite of both the Greeks and the Romans who considered that the two halves of the nut resembled the two lobes of the brain, and therefore would make a good remedy for headaches, or might even boost brain-power. Walnut oil was especially appreciated – then as now.

Thought to be originally a native of the shores of the Caspian Sea, the walnut tree gradually spread up into Europe and was in due course exported to America. In the States it is known as the English walnut, to distinguish it from the native American black walnut (*Juglans nigra*) which has a much harder shell. Though walnuts are now extensively cultivated, the tree is still to be found growing wild in many parts of Europe, often on roadsides or at the edge of fields.

The walnut is one of the last of the deciduous trees to come into leaf. Because it is rather vulnerable to late frosts, it seldom fruits satisfactorily in northerly parts of Europe. Even in Alsace we hold our breath each year until the Ice Saints have passed, the three saints' days in mid-May after which there is no more danger of frosts. A few degrees below zero when the tree is just daring to show a little growth brings blackened branch tips and there will be no walnuts for the autumn. After the catkins (male and female are produced on the same tree), the fruit gradually takes shape, pale green ovals at the tips of the branches, which slowly swell until they reach maturity in the autumn.

Once ripe, the walnut is catapulted from its green casing and falls to the ground with a satisfying thud. Freshly fallen from the tree, the nuts are rather grubby and encased in a network of black threads which stain your fingers better than any black dye – rubber gloves are indicated. They need a good

scrubbing before being laid out to dry. Outside Paulette's old barn, the walnuts are laid out in big wooden sieves and boxes, cocked up to catch the last rays of the dying autumn sun. If stored before the shells are fully dry, she tells me, they soon go mouldy.

The new season's walnuts can be separated from their thin tannic film by scalding them in boiling water – an important step for delicate sauces such as that used in the beautiful Mexican dish *chiles en nogada*, stuffed chillies or sweet peppers cloaked in a virginal creamy-white walnut sauce and splattered with the blood-red specks of pomegranate seeds.

In peasant economies where walnuts grow plentifully, nothing is wasted. The leaves are made into a liqueur; the green nuts are made into jam, or steeped in eau-de-vie and/or wine, sweetened and spiced. The British treatment is more brutal, pickling them in vinegar with onion, garlic and spices. The ripe nuts are traditional autumn fare in Alsace served with bacon and washed down with the rather hazardous still-fermenting wine (*Neia Siassa*).

A surfeit of nuts can be made into oil, which they contain in abundance. They are thus extremely fattening (or nutritious, depending on your point of view). Up in the Vosges in the St Amarin valley, a local physics teacher and two carpenters recently resurrected an old oil mill which is now in working order. Anyone with a good crop of walnuts can take them there to be ground. Don't squirrel away the oil for too long: enjoy it while you may for it quickly goes rancid.

WHOLEWHEAT BREAD WITH WALNUTS

If making two loaves, double everything except the yeast.

MAKES 1 LOAF

300g/10oz strong white bread flour (US 2-2½ cups all-purpose flour)
100g/3½oz (US ¾ cup) wholewheat flour
100g/3½oz (US 1 cup) rye flour
12 walnuts, shelled and roughly chopped
2 tsp salt
15g/1½oz fresh yeast or 1 packet (7g/¼oz) fast-action dried yeast (US 1 package rapid-rise dry yeast)
2 tbsp walnut oil
125ml/4floz plain yogurt
about 200ml/7floz warm water

In a large bowl (or the bowl of the electric mixer, with a dough hook) mix together the flours, walnuts and salt. Crumble in the fresh yeast, or sprinkle on the dried. Add the oil, yogurt and water, mix and knead by hand, or with the machine, until the dough is firm and comes away from the sides of the bowl and/or your hands. If still very soft, add sprinkles of the flour as necessary. Encase the bowl in a plastic bag and leave the dough to rise at room temperature for 2 hours or until doubled in bulk.

Knock the dough down. Shape into a round loaf, put it on a small, well-floured board and make a cross cut in the top; or roll it up into a bolster and put in an oiled loaf pan. Leave for 30 minutes to rise again. Heat the oven to 220°C/425°F/Gas 7. Place a floured baking tray inside. Shunt the round loaf off its board on to the heated tray, or put the loaf pan in the oven. Bake for 15 minutes, then lower the heat to 180°C/350°F/Gas 4 for 30 minutes or until nut brown and the loaf sounds hollow when inverted and tapped.

COUNTRY TERRINE WITH WALNUTS

A basic pork, veal and liver forcemeat is processed fairly coarsely and layered in a terrine with walnuts. Be sure to make it at least a week before it is needed, so that the flavours have time to mature.

MAKES A TERRINE GIVING 16 SLICES

300g/10oz lean boneless pork
300g/10oz lean boneless veal
300g/10oz liver: chicken, pig's, lamb's
300g/10oz fresh pork back fat
2 level tsp salt
½ level tsp mixed spice (US apple pie spice)
pepper

finely grated zest of ½ orange
a pinch dried or fresh thyme
6 juniper berries, crushed
2 tbsp Madeira or Port
optional, but desirable: a piece of caul fat large enough to line the terrine
12 walnut halves
a bayleaf

Trim the well-chilled meats and fat of all tendon, membrane or gristle and chop roughly. Process to a sausage-meat texture in the food processor with the salt, spice, pepper to taste, zest and herbs. Stir in the Madeira or Port and the crushed juniper berries. Chill the mixture.

If using caul fat, soak it in warm water if necessary to make it pliable, then use it to line a 26 × 8 × 8cm/ 10½ × 3½ × 3½ inch terrine or loaf pan. Using wet hands, press half the forcemeat into the terrine and smooth the surface. Press the walnut halves on top, then cover with the remaining forcemeat, pressing down well to make sure there are no air spaces. Bring the caul fat up and over the top to enclose and top with a bayleaf. Cover with foil and a lid if available.

Put a folded sheet of newspaper in a roasting pan (stops splashback and prevents violent heat shocks to the bottom of the terrine) and put the terrine on top. Pour in boiling water to come two-thirds of the way up the sides of the terrine. Bake for 1¼ hours in a 180°C/350°F/Gas 4 oven. Then remove the foil and lid, raise the heat to 200°C/400°F/Gas 6 and bake for a further 15-20 minutes to brown the top. The terrine is done when slightly shrunk from the sides and feels firm and springy to the touch, not at all squashy.

Leave to cool, then refrigerate for 5-6 days. Serve slices direct from the dish, with plenty of good bread and sweet-sour cherries (page 53) or chutney.

Lasagne of Field Mushrooms and Leeks with a Walnut Sauce

A creamy walnut sauce with a hint of garlic goes well with this sumptuous vegetarian pasta dish of field mushrooms and leeks. It could also be served as an accompaniment to plainly roasted or grilled chicken.

SERVES 8

AS A MAIN COURSE, PROBABLY 12 AS A VEGETABLE ACCOMPANIMENT

2 cloves garlic, mashed
1 large onion, finely chopped
50g / scant 2oz (US 3¹/₂ tbsp)
*   butter*
1.2kg / 2lb 10oz field
*   mushrooms, sliced*
salt and pepper
4-5 tbsp sour cream or crème
*   fraîche*
several sprigs tarragon, chopped
600g / 1¹/₄lb leeks, sliced about
*   1cm / ³/₈ inch thick*
125ml / 4floz water

1 clove garlic, peeled but left
*   whole*
1 tbsp oil
100g / 3¹/₂oz (US 1¹/₃ cups)
*   ground walnuts*
200ml / 7floz dry white wine
200ml / 7floz whipping cream
*   (US heavy cream)*
16 sheets lasagne: about
*   250g / 9oz*
8 tbsp fromage frais
3 tbsp grated Parmesan

Soften the garlic and onion in half the butter until golden. Add the mushrooms, season to taste and cover. Cook gently for 5-6 minutes or until the juices are released. Uncover, raise the heat and allow the juices to evaporate. Stir in the cream, bubble up and cook for a few minutes more. Stir in the herbs. Set aside.

Put the sliced leeks in a wide, shallow pan with the water, remaining butter, and salt and pepper to taste. Cook rather briskly for about 10 minutes or until the water evaporates and the leeks are barely tender. Set aside.

Fry the garlic clove in the hot oil until golden and the oil well flavoured. Remove the garlic and stir in the ground nuts. Add the wine and cream and simmer gently for 15 minutes. If too thick loosen the sauce with a little water or stock.

If necessary, blanch the lasagne sheets in boiling salted water, drain and refresh in cold water. Lift them on to a teatowel and pat them dry. Lightly butter an ovenproof dish. Put half the mushrooms in the bottom. Follow with a layer of lasagne sheets, then half the leeks and 4 tbsp *fromage frais*. Repeat the layers, finishing with a layer of lasagne. Top with the walnut sauce and grated Parmesan. Bake at 180°C / 350°F / Gas 4 for about 25 minutes or until thoroughly hot.

STUFFED HOT-SWEET PEPPERS WITH A CREAMY WALNUT SAUCE

This adaptation of the classic Mexican recipe *chiles en nogada* is uniquely suited to wild foodies with access to the new season's walnuts. Only when freshly harvested can the thin membrane covering the nuts be easily removed. This dish had a startling effect on the wedding guests in the delightful book (and film) *Like water for chocolate* by Laura Esquivel. Once you have eaten it you may understand why.

SERVES 6

6 green sweet peppers
1 tbsp oil
600 g / 1¼ lb minced beef (US ground beef), or mixed beef and pork
1 large onion, chopped
3 cloves garlic, mashed
4 fresh hot green chillies, seeded and finely chopped
3 large tomatoes; about 500 g / 1 lb 2 oz, skinned and chopped
4 cloves
1 tsp cumin seeds
1 tsp black peppercorns
a 1 cm / ³⁄₈ inch piece cinnamon stick
4 tbsp raisins or sultanas (US golden raisins)

3 tbsp chopped almonds
1 pear, cored and finely chopped
1 apple, cored and finely chopped
salt
2 thick slices white bread: about 50 g / scant 2 oz, crusts removed, chopped
about 24 large fresh walnuts: to give 125 g / 4½ oz walnut flesh
200 ml / 7 fl oz double cream (US heavy cream) or crème fraîche
125 g / 4½ oz low fat cream cheese: St. Moret light or similar
about 100 ml / 3½ fl oz milk
seeds from ½ pomegranate

Turn the peppers under a fierce grill (US broiler) or over a gas flame until evenly and thoroughly blackened and blistered. Wrap them in a teatowel and put them into a large plastic bag while you prepare the filling.

Heat the oil and cook the minced meat over high heat, turning until browned in parts and no longer raw-looking. Lift out the meat with a slotted spoon and set it aside. Discard all but 1 tbsp fat. Soften the onion, garlic and chillies in this fat without allowing them to brown. Add the tomatoes and cook down to a thick consistency. Grind the cloves, cumin seed, peppercorns and cinnamon stick in a mortar or spice mill. Add them to the pan with the raisins or sultanas, almonds, pear and apple. Return the meat to the pan and stir everything well together. Season to taste. Cook over gentle heat for 10-15 minutes to allow the flavours to fuse together.

Rub the charred skin off the peppers under running water. Make an incision down one side of each and carefully pull out the seeds without removing the stalk or otherwise breaking the flesh. Fill the peppers with the meat mixture. Place them seam side down in an ovenproof dish and cover with foil. (The dish may be prepared ahead to this point and refrigerated or frozen.)

To make the sauce, reduce the bread cubes to crumbs in a food processor. Cover the walnut halves with boiling water and leave for 5 minutes. Then peel away the brown membrane. Put the nuts in cold water as they are peeled, to prevent them discolouring. When they are all ready, put them in the food processor with the crumbs. Add the cream and cream cheese and process until smooth, adding only enough milk to give a soft pouring consistency. Do not overdo it or you risk curdling the sauce. Set aside.

Heat the stuffed peppers in a 180°C / 350°F / Gas 4 oven for 15-20 minutes. Spoon the cold sauce over them just before serving and sprinkle with pomegranate seeds.

CHESTNUT

CASTANEA SATIVA

F: Marron, châtaigne. G: Kastanie. When the weather turns cold you set off for a brisk country walk, rustling through the golden leaves shed by the graceful old chestnut trees lining the stony tracks through the woods. Excitement mounts as among the leaves you stumble upon some half-open prickly parcels lying on the ground. You bear them home triumphantly, anticipating a feast. Gradually the awful truth dawns: while the chestnut is neatly packaged, it is certainly not a convenience food, and far from fast. First you struggle with the prickles, then you battle with the leathery inner skin. Later you burn your fingers as you attempt to peel the nuts. But it's worth it in the end. Chestnuts have a wonderful, winter warming quality. What a good thing they come into season when the temperature drops and calorific food seems to be what you need (or at least what you want).

The sweet chestnut (not to be confused with the horse chestnut, *Aesculus hippocastanum*, unpalatably bitter but good for playing the British children's game of conkers) originated in Asia Minor and grows wild throughout most of Europe and in some parts of North America. In Europe, there seems to be a great swathe of chestnut groves from Portugal through Spain and across the Pyrenees to southwestern France, the Ardèche, Savoie, southern Switzerland (especially Ticino), Italy and Greece. Unfussy about soil, the chestnut tree does however need a certain amount of summer sun followed by autumn rain for the nuts to swell. For the existence of sweet chestnut trees up in cool, temperate Britain, it seems we have the Romans to thank.

Chestnut wood has a wonderful colour and fine grain and has long been a favourite of coopers and cabinetmakers. On a less exalted level it was also used for pit props and for telegraph poles. Those who unthinkingly cut down chestnut groves for wood without a re-planting programme do so at their peril: it will be at least twenty years before the tree fruits, and many more before the trunk is fully mature. The chestnut tree can live for several hundred years. Bees buzz happily between its leathery leaves and make from its flowers a rich, mahogany-coloured honey with a powerful and distinctive flavour. The spear-shaped, serrated leaves are used in what the French call *la médicine douce* (alternative or complementary medicine). Even the catkin-like flowers are made into fritters.

But for most people it is the nuts, high in starch and low in oil, which are the crucial crop. The chestnut has been to poor southern areas as the potato to the north. In times of hardship it became a staple food, ground up into flour and used in breads, cakes and porridge-like broths, or whole in place of meat. Hard as it is nowadays to imagine the Italian-speaking part of Switzerland (the Ticino) as anything other than incredibly prosperous and impeccably groomed, as recently as the Thirties it was a rudely poor area in which *la castagña* formed the backbone of the people's diet. Nowadays there is scant evidence of the crucial role it once played. Chic visitors to the annual *castagnata* or chestnut festival beneath the arcades of Morcote beside Lake Lugano each autumn are probably oblivious of the whole Ticino chestnut tradition as they nibble at hot chestnuts and down a *tazzin* or two of local Merlot.

If you have only ever had shop-bought, cultivated chestnuts, you are in for a surprise when you open up a wild one. More often than not the prickly round parcel (which if ripe will already have burst open to reveal the contents) will contain not one dark brown shiny nut but two or three small flat ones. In some languages (notably the ones in which chestnuts are familiar fare), there is a nominal distinction: in French, for instance, the small chestnuts are *châtaignes* and the large ones (usually from grafted trees) *marrons*.

A prerequisite for peeling chestnuts is a good group of kind friends who have a vested interest in the end result. Having found your nuts and divested them of their prickly husks, assemble your helpers in the kitchen. Hand out the small sharp knives and have everyone make a cut in the leathery skin around the waist of each nut. Then either bake them in a hot oven for 10-15 minutes, or cover them with water and boil them for 5-10 minutes. As the nuts begin to burst open, remove them a few at a time from the heat with a slotted spoon. Equipped with rubber gloves (they must be peeled while still hot) and a small sharp knife, peel away the skin and the inner membrane. Sometimes this will come away with the leathery skin; sometimes you must insist a little, or even return the nut to the pan for reheating. Beware the explosive qualities of chestnuts, either in the fire (hence the need to puncture the skin first) or in the body (cook them thoroughly in water or stock).

From about 700 g / 1 lb 9 oz whole, large chestnuts you should get about 500 g / 1 lb 2 oz peeled – rather less if they are the tiny flat ones. Subsequent cooking can be in water, stock, milk or sugar syrup. Some Périgord cooks wrap them in a parcel of blanched cabbage leaves and then simmer them in water, to stop them sticking to the bottom of the pan and disintegrating. Their affinity with game or rich meats such as pork, goose or duck is well documented; remember that they are high in starch but low in fat, so while they make good partners for fatty foods, I think it's best to avoid combining them with other carbohydrates (like pasta or potatoes). Mashed or processed with a little butter, they make a marvellous purée – not unlike Mexican pinto bean purée both in colour and in texture, and with the same applications.

Of the sweet chestnut confections, there is the awe-inspiring, cream-laden Monte Bianco or Mont Blanc (depending on which side of the Alps you come from); the Swiss *vermicelles*, spiralling piles of chestnut purée resembling worm casts; and countless chestnut ices and cakes. Perhaps the best known chestnut sweetmeats are the rather wonderful marrons glacés which are the speciality of Privas in the Ardèche region of France. They were a favourite food of Nöel Coward's who recommended them as the ideal remedy for workout freaks and fanatic joggers. 'Exercise', he commented, 'is the most awful illusion. The secret is a lot of aspirin and marrons glacés.'

CHESTNUT SOUP

Because wild chestnuts are often rather small, flat and puny, it's a good idea to put them into a soup. If you have a rich and well flavoured game or turkey stock to hand, the soup will be the better for it.

SERVES 6

1 onion, finely chopped
1 clove garlic
1 stalk celery, chopped, or a piece celeriac (US celery root), peeled and chopped
25g / scant 1oz (US 1½ tbsp) butter
500g / 1lb 2oz peeled chestnuts

1.5 litres / 2⅓ pints (US 1½ quarts) chicken, turkey or game stock, or water +3 chicken stock cubes
salt and pepper
a sprig winter savory or lovage
sour cream, fromage frais or Greek yogurt

Soften the onion, garlic and celery gently in the butter. Add the chestnuts and turn them in the hot butter for a few minutes. Add the stock, salt and pepper to taste and savory or lovage. Bring to the boil, then cover and simmer gently for 30-35 minutes or until the chestnuts are quite soft.

Fish out the herb and liquidize the soup until smooth. Return it to the pan, check the seasoning and serve with a blob of sour cream (or alternative) on each serving.

CHESTNUTS WITH SMOKED SAUSAGES

The floury sweetness of the chestnut is offset by the rich smokey flavours of the sausage in this dish. A sharply dressed orange salad with some finely chopped (purple) onion makes a nice foil.

SERVES 4

700g / 1lb 9oz chestnuts: to give about 500g / 1lb 2oz when peeled
1 onion, finely chopped
25g / scant 1oz (US 1½ tbsp) butter
300ml / 10floz chicken stock or water + ½ chicken stock cube

juice 1 orange
salt and pepper
a bouquet garni
4 smoked boiling sausages: about 400g / 14oz

Peel the chestnuts as directed above. Soften the onion in the butter without allowing it to brown. Add the chestnuts, tossing them to coat with butter. Add the stock and orange juice, season to taste and add the bouquet garni. Simmer for about 25 minutes or until just cooked. If you like your chestnuts a little firm, not mushy, this should be long enough if they are freshly fallen.

Slice the sausages into chestnut-sized chunks, add them to the pan and simmer together for a further 5-10 minutes until they are good and hot.

CHESTNUTS WITH HORNS OF PLENTY

The intensely perfumed Horns of Plenty (see page 108) combine beautifully with the smooth floury nuts. For lack of these, any other mushroom (wild or cultivated) could be substituted. A good dish to serve with game.

SERVES 4

1 onion, finely chopped
1 clove garlic, crushed
25g / scant 1oz (US 1½tbsp) butter
a handful Horns of Plenty or other mushrooms
salt and pepper

500g / 1lb 2oz peeled chestnuts
300ml / 10floz chicken or beef stock, or water + ½ stock cube
2 tbsp Port or other fortified wine
a bayleaf

Soften the onion and garlic in the butter, then add the Horns of Plenty or other mushrooms and salt and pepper to taste. Cover the pan and cook gently for 5 minutes. Add the chestnuts, turning them in the fat. Add the stock, Port or other wine and the bay leaf. Bring to the boil and simmer for 25-30 minutes or until the nuts are just tender.

CHESTNUT AND ORANGE CUSTARD WITH CHOCOLATE SAUCE

CHESTNUT AND ORANGE CUSTARD WITH CHOCOLATE SAUCE

Serve with a chocolate sauce made by melting 150g / 5oz dark chocolate in 250ml / 8floz water with 100g / 3½oz (US ½ cup) sugar and simmering until thick and syrupy.

SERVES 6-8

400g / 14oz peeled chestnuts
grated zest of 1 and juice of 2 oranges
2-3 tbsp water
½ tsp powdered vanilla, or 1 tsp vanilla essence (US vanilla extract)

100g / 3½oz (US ½ cup) sugar
4 eggs
500ml / 16floz hot milk
some walnut halves to garnish
sweetened whipped cream

Put the chestnuts in a pan with the orange zest and juice, water, vanilla and 3 tbsp of sugar. Cover and simmer for 10-15 minutes until soft. Mash the nuts with a potato masher, or process them roughly in the food processor.

Heat the oven to 180°C / 350°F / Gas 4. Process or whisk together the remaining sugar, eggs and hot milk, then add the chestnut purée. Pour into a buttered 1.5 litre / 2⅓ pint (US 1½ quart) charlotte mould or soufflé dish. Place in a roasting pan with water to come halfway up the sides of the mould or dish and bring the water almost to the boil on top of the stove. Bake in the pre-heated oven for 1-1½ hours – the custard will cook quicker in a metal charlotte mould than in a ceramic soufflé dish. Stick a skewer in the middle – it should come out clean, and the custard should not be unduly wobbly.

Cool in the mould or dish. Slip a knife around it and turn it out. Decorate with walnut halves and serve whipped cream and chocolate sauce separately.

CHIVES

ALLIUM SCHOENOPRASUM

F: Ciboulette. G: Schnittlauch. Chives, from the allium family (of which onions and garlic are also members), grow wild throughout Europe and survive eastwards as far as Siberia. They would need to be tough to survive the Siberian climate. Even in this eastern part of France, where we can have quite fearsome winters (at least by European standards), they soldier valiantly on in sub-zero temperatures, pushing their tender green spikes up out of the snow, and later through the yellow, winter-tired grass. To my great delight they flourish throughout our area: I have found them on grassy banks, in pastures, in the vineyards (where they seem to be especially at home) and – most convenient of all – in the abandoned orchard behind our house. As the days lengthen and the temperature rises, the spikes become quite tubular, tougher and darker – almost like spring onions. Later, when the meadow is mown for hay or the banks cut, they disappear entirely from the landscape and you wonder if they were ever really there, or if you just dreamt it.

In the early part of the year they are especially welcome at a time when not much else is moving in the wild, and particularly not in the herb line. Traditionally valued as an appetite sharpener and an aid to reducing high blood pressure, they are most welcome as an important source of vitamins (notably C, B1 and B2).

The flavour of wild chives is more robust than that of their cultivated cousins, but recipes are interchangeable. It is well known (but bears repeating) that chives should not be cooked, properly speaking, but simply sprinkled over almost cooked dishes or into sauces, otherwise the flavour is lost. They are excellent snipped into a crêpe batter to give a flecked green and mildly oniony result; lengths of wild chives, being tougher, are effective for tying up crêpe parcels or securing bundles of beans. Unfortunately, wild chives do not seem to produce the lovely mauve flowers of the cultivated variety, which make such a nice garnish, dismembered and scattered over salads.

CHIVE-SPECKLED CRÊPES

Chopped chives added to a crêpe batter gives a beautiful green and speckled effect and all the taste of the herb is conserved in the brief cooking they get. Wrap them around a delicious filling, or make them into parcels or purses as in the following recipes; or use them in your own creations.

MAKES 8-9 CRÊPES ABOUT 22 CM / 9 INCHES IN DIAMETER OR 10-12 CRÊPES ABOUT 18 CM / 7 INCHES IN DIAMETER OR 16 CRÊPES ABOUT 15 CM / 6 INCHES IN DIAMETER

125 ml / 4 fl oz water	2 eggs
125 ml / 4 fl oz milk	1 tsp salt
100 g / 3½ oz (US ⅔ cup) flour	chives
2 tbsp oil	

Put the water, milk, flour, oil, eggs and salt in the blender. You could use the food processor but the chives will blend in less well and the batter will not be a good green colour. Snip plenty of chives over the top and blend or process to a speckled green batter. Scrape down the sides and re-blend if necessary. Leave the batter to rest to allow the starch cells to swell, which gives a lighter, finer crêpe.

Brush out a heavy crêpe pan or frying pan with a little oil. Heat to almost smoking, then pour in only enough batter to coat the bottom of the pan very thinly. Any excess batter should be immediately tipped back into the blender. Cook until the underside is golden, then flip the crêpe over and cook the second side till lightly spotty. Stack them up as they are finished. If not to be used immediately, wrap in a teatowel, put in a plastic bag and refrigerate. Or freeze in foil.

FISH PAVÉS WITH CREAMY CHIVE SAUCE

Salmon works well in this dish, the pink of the fish contrasting with the green crêpes.

SERVES 8

8 square slabs of fish: salmon, halibut, monkfish, turbot etc, each about 150 g / 5 oz (a 2 kg / 4½ lb salmon will give you about 1.3 kg / 2 lb 14 oz skinned fillets, enough for 8 slabs)	25 g / scant 1 oz (US 1½ tbsp) butter
salt and pepper	250 ml / 8 fl oz white wine
8 chive-speckled crêpes at least 20 cm / 8 inches in diameter (opposite)	250 ml / 8 fl oz fish or chicken stock, or water + ½ chicken or fish stock cube
olive oil	1 tsp cornflour (US cornstarch) mixed with a little water
1 shallot, finely chopped	200 ml / 7 fl oz whipping cream (US heavy cream) or crème fraîche
	a bunch chives, finely snipped

Season the fish lightly. Place each slab in the middle of a crêpe (speckled side uppermost), fold the sides and ends up to make a neat parcel, and place seam sides down on a baking sheet. Refrigerate if not to be baked at once.

Make the sauce: soften the shallot in the butter. Add the wine, reduce by half, then add the stock and reduce again by half. Stir in the cornflour, add the cream and simmer for 5-10 minutes or until lightly thickened.

Heat the oven to 220°C / 425°F / Gas 7. Brush the parcels with olive oil and bake for 7-8 minutes or until the fish feels firm and springy. The parcels should be golden.

Reheat the sauce and stir in the chives. Simmer briefly. Pour a little sauce on to each heated plate, place a parcel on top and garnish with crossed swords of chives.

Spinach Money Bags with a Spicy Tomato Sauce

Chive-speckled crêpes are filled with a lightly cheesy spinach mixture, made into money bags and their necks tied with chives for a chic first course – or serve two per person for a light lunch. It's a fiddly dish, but worth it for the effect. The bags can be prepared well in advance of the meal and refrigerated or frozen.

SERVES 8

FOR A STARTER OR 4 FOR A LIGHT MEAL

500g/1lb 2oz fresh spinach, or
  250g/9oz frozen
salt
12g/¹/₂oz (US 1 tbsp) butter
1 tbsp flour
125ml/4floz milk
pepper
2 tbsp cream
2 tbsp grated Parmesan
8 chive-speckled crêpes at least
  22cm/9 inches in diameter
  (page 129)

16 long, strong chives to tie the
  purses
1 × 400g/14oz can peeled
  tomatoes with their juice
1 shallot or small onion, chopped
2-4 fresh hot green chillies,
  seeded and chopped
1 clove garlic, mashed
a pinch sugar
1 tbsp oil
optional: sour cream or fromage
  frais

Cook fresh spinach in minimal salted water, drain, refresh in cold water and squeeze dry. (Alternatively, thaw and squeeze dry frozen spinach.) Chop either sort roughly. Heat the butter and toss the spinach in it. Sprinkle on the flour and cook for a couple of minutes, stirring to mix well. Add the milk and boil to thicken the mixture. Season with pepper and add the cream and Parmesan.

Put a mound of spinach in the middle of each crêpe, speckled side uppermost, golden side under. Bring the edges of each crêpe up to form a money bag and tie at the neck with a double length of chives. Put them on a baking sheet lined with non-stick paper. (Can be refrigerated or frozen until needed.)

For the sauce, blend or process together the tomatoes, shallot or onion, chillies, garlic, a pinch of salt and sugar. Heat the oil in a heavy pan, throw in the purée and cook briskly, stirring, for a few minutes. Reduce the heat and simmer for 30 minutes. Push the sauce through a sieve. Return it to the pan for reheating later.

Heat the oven to 200°C/400°F/Gas 6. Brush the money bags with a little olive oil and bake for 10-12 minutes until golden brown and a little crispy. Put a little hot sauce on each plate, the money bag on top and a splash of sour cream beside.

DICED SALMON AND MUSHROOMS WITH CHIVES AND RÖSTI

When salmon is cheap (which, in these days of farmed fish, it increasingly is), pounce on it, fillet and skin it, and use some for this delectable quickie supper dish for 2. Or double the quantities and invite some good friends for a chic supper in the kitchen – not a dinner party dish, as it is a last-minute affair.

SERVES 2

500g/1lb 2oz firm potatoes
salt and pepper
olive oil
300g/10oz skinless, boneless
   fillet of salmon, diced
flour
1 shallot, finely chopped
150g/5oz mushrooms, roughly
   chopped

juice ½ lime or 1 lime
200ml/7floz white wine
200ml/7floz stock or water
200ml/7floz whipping cream
   (US heavy cream)
plenty of chopped chives

For the *Rösti*, cook the potatoes for 15 minutes in salted water. Drain, refresh and cool them. Peel and grate on a coarse cheese grater. Season with salt and pepper. Heat a film of oil in a non-stick pan. Tip the grated potatoes into the hot oil and press them down firmly and neatly with the back of a wooden spoon. Cook for 8-10 minutes or until the underside is golden. Turn out on to a plate, heat a little more oil and shunt the *Rösti* back into the pan to cook the other side.

Dust the diced salmon in seasoned flour; shake off excess flour in a colander. Heat a film of oil in a non-stick pan until almost smoking. Toss in the salmon cubes and cook for 1 minute or until just golden and a little crusty, then turn them over to cook the other side. Remove with a slotted spoon and keep warm.

Lower the heat. Soften the shallot (in a little more oil if necessary) without allowing it to brown. Add the mushrooms, salt, pepper and lime or lemon juice. Cover and cook gently for 5 minutes, then uncover, raise the heat and cook briskly to evaporate the juices. Add the wine and stock or water and boil hard to reduce the liquid to just a few tablespoonsful. Add the cream and simmer gently for 5 minutes.

Return the salmon to the pan, stir in the chives, bubble up and serve at once on heated plates with the *Rösti*.

132

HORSERADISH

ARMORACIA RUSTICANA

F: Raifort. G: Meerettich. Horseradish suffers from an image problem. The 'horse' prefix (denoting inferiority, as in horse chestnut or horse mushroom) is enough to give it a complex. A perennial plant with tall, tapering rough green leaves, the root looks like a parsnip gone wrong. It thrives on rough ground – and is better left there. Many an unwary gardener has gratefully accepted a plant from a well-wishing (?) neighbour, only to find that it has invaded the plot. The German name ('sea-radish') is a bit kinder; the French (at least the non-*alsaciens*) refer to it as *moutarde des allemands* (German mustard) and describe it darkly as a *condiment brutal*.

A native of eastern Europe, horseradish is still extensively used east of the Rhine, and in the German-speaking part of Switzerland. But it is probably the chefs of Alsace who have done the most for its reputation. Here the marriage of east European ingredients with French savoir-faire often produces outstanding results – as witnessed in Antoine Westermann's (Restaurant Buerehiesel, Strasbourg) mousselines of pike with creamy horseradish sauce, or the bacon-larded salmon steaks on a bed of horseradish-flavoured lentils from Michel Husser of Le Cerf in Marlenheim. The Scandinavians likewise make good use of the root, especially with fish. For many British people, a Sunday lunch of roast beef without horseradish sauce would be like fish without chips.

Horseradish is said to increase the blood flow to skin and tissues – a fact which can readily be believed by the effect it has on the tongue and the sinuses. It is also said to aid digestion and to protect the intestinal tract – apparently it is served with raw fish in Japan as a sort of insurance policy against potential parasites. A salad of cottage cheese with freshly grated horseradish is said to be good for slimmers. (Presumably you would not be tempted to eat much of it.)

Locate the plant by its leaves during the summer – they look a bit like dock leaves, slightly wrinkled. If you pull a bit off and crush it, you will get that unmistakeable, hot horseradish smell. Once the plant is identified, make a mental note so you can return in the autumn to dig up a few roots before it dies back and disappears. If the plant is growing wild, the roots will be brownish yellow, forked and often twisted and hairy. Store them without washing or trimming them in a cool dark place in a box of sand. Otherwise, just when you feel like horseradish sauce the ground is sure to be frozen hard.

To use the root, scrub it, then peel it and grate it – in the food processor with the grating disc if you have one, otherwise you will cry crocodile tears. The closer you get to the heart of the horseradish, the hotter it becomes, so if you want a milder effect grate it down the sides, not across the grain. I like it best when its pungency is tamed by other ingredients – cream, for instance, or apple. Those who relish the sinus-clearing effect will prefer to eat it raw, grated into sour cream or *fromage frais* for eating with cold meats, or with a join of hot roast beef, or fish (especially smoked). Once cooked, this ingredient loses most of its ferocious heat, but the subtle horseradish flavour lingers on.

To make your own horseradish cream (similar to bottled horseradish sauce but much more pungent), add 2 tbsp of the grated root to 6-7 tbsp sour cream or *crème fraîche*, a little lemon juice, and salt and pepper. Covered, it will keep in the fridge for several days. Horseradish butter can be made in the same way as wild garlic butter (page 35) and refrigerated or frozen. True gluttons for punishment may like to try horse-radish vinegar, made on the same principle as herb vinegars (page 70).

POTATO SALAD WITH HORSERADISH AND WALNUT SAUCE

Horseradish and walnuts are often combined in recipes, particularly to go with fish. Here is a nice idea for a potato salad, which would partner some smoked fish. If possible, use the new season's walnuts (page 117), blanched and divested of their brown, tannic membrane.

SERVES 4-6

1 kg / 2¼ lb waxy potatoes: e.g. Rattes, Désirée, Nicola, Stella
salt and pepper
25 fresh walnuts, shelled and peeled (page 117): to give about 100 g / 3½ oz
2-4 tbsp freshly grated horseradish
juice ½ lemon
250 ml / 8 fl oz sour cream or crème fraîche

Cook the potatoes in their skins until just tender (about 20 minutes, depending on size and type). Drain (keep some of the cooking water), refresh under cold water and peel. Slice and put in a bowl. Season while still warm with salt and pepper. Keep back a few walnuts for the garnish; chop or process the rest fairly finely. Add the grated horseradish, lemon juice, salt, pepper and sour cream or *crème fraîche*. Dilute if necessary to a pouring consistency with some of the potato cooking water or stock. Pour the sauce over the potatoes, turning to coat them well. Scatter the remaining nuts on top.

SMOKED FISH AND HORSERADISH TERRINE

For this terrine you can use smoked mackerel or trout, or an assortment of smoked fish. It sets firmly enough to be cut in slices for serving.

SERVES 6-8

6 sheets gelatine or 1 tbsp powdered unflavoured gelatine
300 ml / 10 fl oz chicken stock or, water + ½ chicken stock cube
300 g / 10 oz skinless, boneless smoked fish
juice ½ lemon
2-4 tbsp freshly grated horseradish
500 ml / 16 fl oz whipping cream (US heavy cream)

Soak the gelatine in cold water until floppy, then squeeze it out and dissolve it gently in the stock. If using powdered gelatine sprinkle it directly on to the stock and leave it to sponge up, then dissolve it gently. Flake the fish into the food processor or blender and pour in the hot gelatine / stock mixture, the lemon juice and 2 tbsp horseradish. Process until smooth. Taste and add more horseradish if you wish. (Check the seasoning: the fish is usually salty enough, and the horseradish will provide the peppery element.) Cool the fish mixture.

Whip the cream to soft peaks. Fold 300 ml / 10 fl oz of it into the cooled fish mixture. Pour the mousse into a lightly oiled loaf pan or terrine (26 × 8 × 8 cm / 10½ × 3½ × 3½ inch) and refrigerate until set. Stir the remaining horseradish into the rest of the whipped cream and season to taste. Slice the terrine and serve with a little oval of horseradish cream.

GRATIN OF HAM WITH A CREAMY HORSERADISH VELOUTÉ

An excellent way to use up slices of leftover Christmas ham or gammon. Serve with baked potatoes and a winter salad of chicory (US Belgian endive), lamb's lettuce and curly endive. If you want the heat of horseradish as well as its flavour, keep back a little to add freshly grated to the finished sauce.

SERVES 4-6

800g-1.2kg / 1¾-2lb 10oz cooked ham or gammon, sliced thickly
25g / scant 1oz (US 1½ tbsp) butter
2 tbsp flour
200ml / 7fl oz milk
200ml / 7fl oz ham stock, or water + ½ chicken stock cube
2 tbsp cream
2-3 tbsp freshly grated horseradish
salt
lemon juice

Put the slices of ham or gammon in an ovenproof dish, overlapping them slightly. Melt the butter over high heat, stir in the flour and allow to cook for a few minutes. Add the milk and stock and bring to the boil, stirring the while. Enrich with the cream, spike with the horseradish, and sharpen with salt and a few drops lemon juice. Simmer for 10 minutes.

Pour the sauce over the ham or gammon and bake in a 200°C / 400°F / Gas 6 oven for 20-25 minutes or until golden and bubbly, and thoroughly hot. (Alternatively, heat in a combination microwave oven with top heat following the manufacturer's instructions.)

WARM SALAD OF LENTILS WITH SMOKED HADDOCK AND HORSERADISH

A nice little lentil stew is served just warm with smoked fish and a spicy dressing.

SERVES 4

200g / 7oz (US 1 cup) green lentils, soaked overnight
grated zest and juice ½ lemon
1 onion, finely chopped
500ml / 16fl oz water
pepper
salt
2 tbsp walnut oil
4 tbsp tasteless oil
2 tbsp wine vinegar or lemon juice
1 tsp sugar
3 tbsp cream
freshly grated horseradish to taste
300g / 10oz smoked haddock fillet (US finnan haddie)
a bayleaf
radiccio leaves
chives or snipped rocket leaves (US arugula)

Cook the drained lentils with the lemon juice and zest, onion, water and pepper. Simmer for 40 minutes or until just soft. The liquid should have all but evaporated – if not boil it down to reduce it. Add salt to the lentils.

Whisk together into a smooth dressing the oils, vinegar or lemon juice, sugar, salt, pepper, cream and horseradish to taste (start with 1 tbsp, and add more if you wish). Dress the warm lentils with the horseradish dressing.

Poach the smoked haddock in water with the bayleaf for 5-6 minutes or until opaque. Lift it out, peel away the skin and flake the flesh. Arrange a cupped radiccio leaf on each plate and put some dressed lentils inside. Scatter some haddock pieces on top and sprinkle on chopped chives or rocket leaves.

JUNIPER

JUNIPERUS COMMUNIS

F: Genièvre. G: Wachholder. Juniper bushes thrive throughout most of Europe on even the poorest soils, in highlands as in lowlands. The berries are to the juniper as pine cones to the pine tree. In their first year they are green, and in the autumn of the second they start to show their characteristic bluish-black colour with a grey bloom. They can be harvested in this and subsequent years, and a berry-laden bush (which is female, and needs a neighbouring male in order for it to fruit) will always carry both ripe and unripe berries, enabling you to pick them in succession over the years. Strongly aromatic (especially when crushed), with a smell somewhat reminiscent of turpentine, juniper berries contain a high proportion of invert sugar (30%) and a host of other interesting substances such as pigments, pectin, resins and wax.

Their volatile oils are what gives British gin and Dutch genever their distinctive flavour. Since ancient times the juniper berry has been valued as a diuretic and as an aid to digestion: a handful of berries is an essential adjunct to a dish of *choucroute*, which can put serious strains on the digestive mechanism. They are, on the other hand, contra-indicated for expectant mothers. (A synonym for gin, a much-abused tipple in Victorian Britain, was 'Mother's ruin'.)

In our part of France, juniper branches were sometimes cut (along with holly branches) in lieu of palms for Palm Sunday services. While in some regions, the smoke rising from a juniper fire was thought to keep away evil spirits or to keep the plague at bay, in Alsace the associations are altogether more positive and – as is often the case – gastronomic: juniper branches are extensively used in the smokery because they smoulder gently for a good long time, and impart a wonderful flavour to the home-cured bacons, hams and sausages which are a feature of Alsace cookery. Some people make a *digestif* by macerating the berries (both green and ripe) in eau de vie – the final nail in the coffin after a vast *choucroute*. Since time immemorial, juniper (in the form of oil, tea or wine) has been used to treat rheumatic conditions.

After picking your berries, preferably armed with stout gloves, take them home and dry them slowly in a dark, warm place. Once they are dry, put them in a screwtop jar. For dishes which are briefly cooked, pound them in a pestle and mortar or crush under the flattened blade of a stout knife and then chop finely: this helps to release their volatile oils more quickly. For longer-cooked dishes, like the classic *choucroute*, they can be used whole.

DUCK BREASTS WITH JUNIPER BERRIES IN A GREEN HABIT

Duck breasts are seasoned with the crushed berries and left to marinate before wrapping in a bright green cabbage leaf. Delicious with a gratin of potatoes and ceps (page 92) and some finely shredded green cabbage.

SERVES 4-5

3 duck breasts: about 1kg / 2¼lb with skin	100g / 3½oz (US 7 tbsp) butter
6-8 juniper berries, crushed	1 tsp oil
salt and pepper	300ml / 10 fl oz beef stock, or
a Savoy cabbage: the green, curly-leafed kind	water + ½ beef stock cube
	a bouquet garni
flour	150ml / 5 fl oz red wine

Remove the skin from the duck breasts. (If you wish, you can render the skin down and use the fat for another occasion, and the residual crackling (*grattons*) to toss over a salad.) Season the duck breasts with the juniper berries and salt and pepper. Leave in a cool place for a few hours, or overnight.

Remove some bright green, undamaged outer leaves from the cabbage, cut each one in two lobes and remove the hard central rib. Blanch them in boiling water for 2 minutes. They should be just limp. Drain, refresh them in cold water to set the colour and lay on a teatowel to dry.

Cut the breasts in half and wrap or fold them in the leaves, ribbed side inside. Fix with toothpicks if necessary and dust very lightly in flour. Heat a small bit of butter and the oil fiercely in a wide, heavy sauté pan which will take all the breasts in one layer. Fry the parcels briskly until lightly golden – not more than 2 minutes each side. Add the stock and bouquet garni, turn down the heat and simmer for 5 minutes.

Remove the parcels and keep them warm in a low oven. Reduce the stock in the pan by half. Add the red wine and reduce again by half. Discard the bouquet garni. Off the heat, whisk in the remaining butter bit by bit to emulsify the sauce. It will be slightly thickened and glossy. Check the seasoning.

Serve half a breast per person with a little pool of sauce and the chosen vegetable.

DICED GAME WITH RED WINE BUTTER SAUCE AND JUNIPER RÖSTI

Venison (red or roe deer) or wild boar do nicely for this robust winter dish. The *Röstis* are particularly good if made in individual portions.

SERVES 2

500g / 1 lb 2 oz (4-5 medium)	*1 shallot, finely chopped*
firm, waxy potatoes: eg.	*200 ml / 7 fl oz game or beef*
Nicola, Stella, Charlotte	*stock, or water + ½ beef stock*
salt and pepper	*cube*
3 juniper berries, crushed	*100 ml / 3½ fl oz red wine vinegar*
250g / 9 oz diced game	*1 tbsp juniper jelly, or herb jelly*
flour	*(page 72) + 3 more juniper*
100g / 3½ oz (US 7 tbsp) butter	*berries, crushed*
1 tbsp oil	

Make the *Rösti* with the potatoes as described on page 132, but with the addition of the juniper berries.

Toss the diced game in seasoned flour, then shake it vigorously in a colander over the sink to get rid of excess flour. Heat 25g / scant 1oz (US 1½ tbsp) butter and a little oil over good heat in a heavy pan. Fry the meat until a light brown crust forms: keep the meat moving about in the pan – the whole operation should not take more than 5 minutes. Remove the meat and keep it warm; reduce the heat under the pan. Soften the shallot in the same pan (add a little more butter), then add the stock and reduce by half. Add the red wine vinegar and reduce by half again. Whisk in the remaining butter, bit by bit, and the juniper or herb jelly plus juniper berries. You should have 4-5 tbsp rich, well seasoned gamey essence – taste it for seasoning. Put the game back in the pan to heat through. Serve with the *Rösti(s)* on heated plates.

CHICKEN LIVER MOUSSELINE WITH JUNIPER BERRIES

A smooth, rich mousseline with a hint of juniper. Serve with wholewheat bread or toast.

MAKES A 600G / 1¼ LB MOUSSELINE, ENOUGH FOR 6-8

300g / 10 oz chicken livers	*1 clove garlic, crushed*
250 ml / 8 fl oz double cream (US	*2 tbsp Port or sloe gin*
heavy cream) or crème fraîche	*salt and pepper*
50g / scant 2 oz (US 3½ tbsp)	*6-8 juniper berries, crushed*
butter	*a sprig thyme*

Put the chicken livers in the blender or food processor with the cream, melted butter, garlic, Port or sloe gin, and salt and pepper to taste. Blend or process until smooth. Push through a sieve to remove any nasties. Stir in the juniper berries. Pour into a 14 × 9 × 6 cm / 5½ × 3½ × 2½ inches terrine and place the thyme sprig on top. Put in a roasting pan with hot water to come halfway up the side of the terrine. Bake in a 180°C / 350°F / Gas 4 oven for 35-40 minutes or until just firm, and a skewer inserted in the middle comes out clean. Cool and then chill the mousseline.

PAUPIETTES OF CHICKEN BREASTS WITH JUNIPER BERRIES AND BACON

Thinly beaten out chicken breasts are seasoned with crushed juniper berries, filled with bacon, walnuts and *fromage frais* or quark, and wrapped in blanched cabbage leaves, paupiette-style. Nice with gnocchi or grated raw potato cakes, plus shredded cabbage lightly cooked with some fine carrot julienne.

SERVES 6

6 chicken breasts (US chicken breast halves): each weighing about 100g / 3¹/₂oz	*6 large green cabbage leaves*
	50g / scant 2oz (US 3¹/₂tbsp) butter
salt and pepper	*300ml / 10floz chicken stock, or*
12 juniper berries, crushed	*water + ¹/₂ chicken stock cube*
a squeeze lemon juice	*1 tsp cornflour (US cornstarch)*
250g / 9oz bacon cubes	*125ml / 4floz single cream (US*
6tbsp chopped walnuts	*light cream)*
6tbsp fromage frais	*finely chopped chives*

Place the chicken breasts between sheets of waxed paper or plastic and beat out gently with a bottle or rolling pin to flatten them slightly. Season with salt, pepper, crushed juniper berries and lemon juice. Leave to marinate while you prepare the filling.

Stew the bacon cubes gently in a heavy pan until the fat runs and they are barely cooked. Do not let them brown. Tip away most of the fat and add the walnuts. Remove from the heat and stir in the *fromage frais* to bind it all together. Taste for seasoning – no salt should be necessary, but maybe a little pepper.

Blanch the cabbage leaves in boiling water for 2 minutes. Cut away the hard central rib and lay them on a teatowel to dry. Place the chicken breasts on top, one to each leaf. Divide the filling among them. Roll up the breasts and lay them seam side down on a board.

About 15 minutes before serving time, melt the butter in a large shallow pan which will take all the breasts in one layer. Put them in seam side down and fry gently for 2 minutes. Turn and fry gently for a further 2 minutes, then add the stock and simmer gently for a final 5 minutes. Remove the breasts to a side dish and keep warm in a low oven. Heat also the serving plates.

Reduce the cooking juices by half to about 200ml / 7floz.

Mix the cornflour into the cream and whisk it into the stock off the heat. Bring back to the simmer and add the chives. Taste for seasoning.

To serve, slice the chicken rolls into 1cm / ³/₈ inch slices and fan them out on the heated plates. Garnish with the chosen accompaniment and pour the sauce around.

LAMB'S LETTUCE OR CORN SALAD

VALERIANELLA LOCUSTA

F: Mâche. G: Nüsslisalat, Feldsalat, Rapunzel. At the tail end of winter, just as I begin to despair of ever finding any wild food again, lamb's lettuce makes its annual appearance. It grows on steep roadside banks, nestling in bare patches of earth among the dormant bramble stems and dead, dried-up tussocks of browned winter grass. They are the same banks where wild chives grow, and where later wild strawberries will appear. Sometimes it grows in crevices in old stone walls. Seldom (if ever) does it grow in meadows. The best sites seem to be vineyards, where I have heard the plant described by winegrowers as *un fléau* – 'a menace'. A more delicious menace would be hard to imagine. In the otherwise dormant winter vineyards of Alsace it grows in profusion, scattering itself at the feet of the gnarled vines and tumbling down over the pink Vosges dry stone walls like soft-edged shooting stars. Down in the market in Colmar in February it costs a fortune. Here it is free for the picking.

Lamb's lettuce (not to be confused with lamb's quarters, another name for fat hen, page 60) is one of the most distinctive and delicious salads to be found in the wild. The plants which you find in February and March have seeded themselves the previous autumn – a situation which the gardener tries to ape in sowing lamb's lettuce in September for harvesting in late autumn and into winter. Because the plant relies on seeding itself in the wild, always leave a few when you pick. A month or two later the tiny flowers (white or pale blue) emerge which will later ripen into seeds about the size of sesame seeds. They are largely deposited in the vicinity of the plant (rather than swept away on the wind) where they bed themselves down for long germination during summer and autumn. Because the seeds stay close to the parent, lamb's lettuce is always to be found in gratifyingly close concentrations, sometimes forming real carpets with intertwining roots. Once the plant has bolted, it is no longer of culinary interest, and becomes bitter and unpalatable.

The familiar names of *Valerianella locusta* are evocative (and/or endearing) in almost any language: one of its English names evokes the soft, floppy ears of the newborn lambs which make their appearance at around the same time of the year; of the French names, *mâche* refers to the nicely ruminative quality of the plant (*mâcher* = to chew), while *doucette*

141

('sweetie') is more affectionate. Because its season invariably falls during Lent, it is sometimes called *salade de chanoine* (and in Spanish *hierba de los canónigos*) – in times when Lent was more strictly observed, the abstemious monks would doubtless have been glad to munch on a little *mâche* to enliven the meatless fast. The Swiss-German term for lamb's lettuce is *Nüsslisalat*, evoking most accurately its wonderful nutty flavour.

It is best to gather lamb's lettuce armed with a sharp little knife. Take a hold of the plant by the leaves and lift it out of the earth a little: the spindly small root will emerge. Cut it off just below the joint between greenery and root, then snip off the root end and any brown or damaged leaves at the base before depositing in basket or bag. (I prefer to leave the plant still attached at the bottom in a nice rosettish cluster, but if there are a lot of dirty or snail-nibbled leaves at the base, you may have to cut off rather a lot and the whole thing will then unravel.) Picking lamb's lettuce is fun; subsequent trimming and cleaning of it is a beastly task and the cook will be grateful if this preliminary preparation is taken care of. Then all that is needed is an energetic swirling in plenty of cold water and a quick spin dry.

LAMB'S LETTUCE SALAD WITH RADICCHIO, RAW MUSHROOMS AND BACON BITS

Good with a quiche for supper.

SERVES 4

about 200g / 7oz trimmed lamb's lettuce	3 tbsp vinegar
	salt and pepper
1 apple-sized radicchio, shredded finely	1 tsp mustard
	150g / 5oz streaky bacon, diced small
200g / 7oz button mushrooms, finely sliced	chopped chives
150ml / 5floz oil	

Mix together on a large, deep plate the lamb's lettuce, radicchio and mushrooms. Shake together the oil, vinegar, salt, pepper and mustard for the dressing and pour it over the salad. Fry the bacon dice in a heavy pan until the fat is rendered and the bacon crisp, lift them out with a slotted spoon and scatter over the salad. Sprinkle on the chopped chives.

LAMB'S LETTUCE SALAD WITH RADICCHIO, RAW MUSHROOMS AND BACON BITS

LAMB'S LETTUCE SALAD WITH BEETROOT, PRAWNS AND PARMESAN DRESSING

A pretty first course salad for the winter months: dark red baby beets on dark green tongues of lamb's lettuce. For the dressing you could use a herb oil (see page 70) with a plain wine vinegar; or a salad oil with a herb vinegar (see page 70). Serve the salad with bread to mop up the dressing.

SERVES 4

1 tsp mustard
salt and pepper
150 ml / 5 fl oz oil
3½ tbsp vinegar
1 tsp honey
2 tbsp freshly grated Parmesan
12 tiny beetroot, no bigger than
  ping pong balls: about
  350 g / 12 oz

1 shallot, finely chopped
2 good handfuls lamb's lettuce:
  about 150 g / 5 oz
15 shelled cooked prawns (US
  shrimp): about 150 g / 5 oz

Make the dressing: whisk or blend together the mustard, 1 tsp salt, plenty of pepper, the oil, vinegar, honey and Parmesan until emulsified.

Put the beetroot in cold water, bring to the boil and cook for 10-15 minutes or until just tender and the skin will rub off easily. Drain, refresh in cold water and rub away skin under running water using rubber gloves. Put the beets in a bowl and toss with some dressing and the chopped shallot while still warm.

Shortly before serving, toss the lamb's lettuce leaves in some more dressing and divide them among four plates. Arrange the beets and prawns on top and drizzle dressing over them.

LAMB'S LETTUCE, CELERY AND WALNUT SALAD WITH AN ORANGE DRESSING

This one works well as a starter or with cold meats.

SERVES 6
AS A FIRST COURSE, 4 AS A SIDE SALAD

about 200 g / 7 oz trimmed
  lamb's lettuce
6 stalks celery, finely sliced

creamy dressing (page 6)
juice of 1 orange
12 walnut halves

Put the lamb's lettuce in a bowl with the celery. Add the orange juice to the creamy dressing and pour enough on to the leaves to coat lightly (the rest can be refrigerated and used for another dish). Sprinkle the nuts on top.

LAMB'S LETTUCE WITH HAM, HORSERADISH AND HARD-BOILED EGGS

A piquant salad of good contrasts.

SERVES 4

100 ml / 3½ fl oz oil
2 tbsp vinegar
salt and pepper
2 tbsp horseradish cream (page
  134, or bottled)
1 tsp sugar

2 tbsp plain yogurt
2 eggs
about 200 g / 7 oz trimmed
  lamb's lettuce
50 g / scant 2 oz cooked ham, cut
  in strips

Blend the oil, vinegar, salt, pepper, horseradish, sugar and yogurt. Boil the eggs for 8 minutes. Drain, refresh in cold water, peel and cut in quarters. Toss the lamb's lettuce in a bowl with the ham and most of the dressing. Arrange the eggs on top and drizzle on more dressing.

MUSSEL

MYTILIS EDULIS

F: Moule. G: (Mies)muschel. Mussels are misunderstood. They have (according to James Laver, quoted in *A Wine and Food Bedside Book*) 'a bad reputation: something mysterious has to be done to them before they can be eaten with safety and no-one seems able to tell one exactly what it is'. The mystery of mussels and what has to be done to them to make them edible seems to be confined to the British Isles; inhabitants of other European nations have fewer hang-ups about this delicious bivalve, which they consume by the ton. Years ago when we were on holiday on the west coast of Scotland, our Spanish cook and her sister let out whoops of joy and *carambas* by the score when they came upon quantities of *mejillones* clinging to the rocks on the shores of Loch Creran. They introduced us to all manner of Spanish mussel-based delights. Thus initiated (and emboldened) we were well equipped when on later holidays we found good infestations on the rocks at low tide in Polzeath. We plucked them by the bucketful and raced back across the bay before the ocean came sweeping in again.

It is nevertheless wise to exercise caution when harvesting your own mussels. The whole mechanics of *Mytilis edulis* and its feeding habits turn it into a potential health hazard. Through its body each day it pumps gallons and gallons of water, taking food for itself and acting as a sort of filter. While the shellfish itself seems to suffer no ill effects from dirty water (indeed mussels are famous for growing fat just beside many a seaside town's outrun of sewage), the more delicate stomachs of humans cannot cope. The mystery about mussels and their preparation revolves therefore around three things: where you pick them (the rocks on which they grow should be far from any outrun of human or other waste products); how vigorous and fresh they are (they should smell only of the sea, and should close up again when tapped smartly); and how and when they are cooked (promptly after harvesting, and briefly – while raw mussels are not to be recommended, overcooking toughens them). Finally, as with all wild foods, take local advice.

Though they occur all the year round, mussels are best picked in cool weather, which makes them ideal winter wild food. Above all, big generous tides are crucial. Not only are the mussels lavishly sluiced at regular intervals with fresh water, but you have a chance to pick them at low tide without getting soaked. It gives another dimension to brisk winter walks on the beach.

When you have gathered your molluscs, put them in a bowl, bucket or basin of cold water. Some people add salt, oatmeal, flour or cornmeal. Leave them for a few hours; change the water and repeat the process. Any which float to the top should be discarded, as should any which are gaping open and remain so even when tapped firmly. Pull out the 'beards' by which they were lately attached to their rock and scrub them with a washing up brush. It is not necessary to remove the barnacles which frequently encrust their dark blue surface.

Put them in a large wide pan, cover and place over high heat. Give them a good shake after a minute or two; after three or four they should have opened up to release a quantity of delicious (but rather salty) juice. Remove them from the heat and tip them (or spoon them) out into a large colander suspended over a bowl. Remove them from the shells. Filter the juice through a fine cloth. Then proceed to use them as directed in the following (or any other) recipes and their juice in sauces or soups. The shells make wonderful compost: put them in a plastic bag, tie the top and jump up and down on them until they are thoroughly broken up.

It is almost impossible to know how much meat you will get from a given quantity of mussels in the shell. At best, from 1 kg / 2¼ lb plump mussels you will probably get about 200 g / 7 oz meat and 300 ml / 10 fl oz juice.

MUSSEL AND BACON QUICHE

A delicious quiche for lunch or supper, the sweet mussel flesh contrasting nicely with the smokey salt bacon. Pick or buy at least 2 kg / 4½ lb mussels in their shells to obtain the quantity of flesh needed.

SERVES 4-6

250 g / 9 oz shortcrust pastry (US basic piecrust)
200 g / 7 oz smoked bacon, cut in small dice
350 g / 12 oz cleaned, cooked and shelled mussels (pages 145-6)
4 eggs
200 ml / 7 fl oz whipping cream (US heavy cream) or crème fraîche
200 ml / 7 fl oz fromage frais, Greek yogurt or plain yogurt
salt and pepper
some crumbled dried herbs

Roll out the pastry to fit a 30 cm / 12 inch quiche tin. Prick the bottom and chill. Fry the bacon cubes gently without extra fat until their own fat is rendered and they are just golden. Tilt the pan to one side and leave it for a few minutes so that the fat runs down, leaving the bacon dry.

Heat the oven to 180°C / 350°F / Gas 4. Lift the bacon out of the pan with a slotted spoon and scatter it with the mussels in the pastry case. Mix together the eggs, cream, *fromage frais* or yogurt, salt and pepper to taste and herbs. Pour it over the bacon and mussels. Bake in the preheated oven for 35-40 minutes or until golden brown and just firm. Cool on a rack.

ROULADE OF MUSSELS

A soufflé base flavoured with mussel juices is baked flat, filled with mussels and *crème fraîche*, and rolled up into a sort of *'moulade'*. It makes a delicious and original starter, served warm or cold, accompanied by a salad of lamb's lettuce and walnuts.

SERVES 4-6

1 kg / 2¹/₄ lb mussels	*100 ml / 3¹/₂ fl oz milk*
25 g / scant 1 oz (US 1¹/₂ tbsp)	*pepper*
butter	*4 eggs, separated*
25 g / scant 1 oz (US 2¹/₂ tbsp)	*3-4 tbsp crème fraîche*
flour	

Clean, cook and shell the mussels as in the general instructions on pages 145-6. You should have about 200 g / 7 oz mussels. Strain the juice through muslin or cheesecloth and set aside 100 ml / 3¹/₂ fl oz of it.

Line a baking sheet 20 × 30 cm / 8 × 12 inches with non-stick baking paper; or make a roulade paper case by cutting out a sheet of non-stick paper 24 × 34 cm / 10 × 14 inches. Fold in 2 cm / ³/₄ inch all around, clip the corners, overlap and fix with staples.

Heat the oven to 180°C / 350°F / Gas 4. Make a soufflé base with the butter, flour, mussel juice, milk and pepper (salt will not be necessary). Remove from the heat and stir in the yolks. Beat the whites to soft peaks and cut and fold them in with a wire whisk. Spread the mixture into the paper case or baking sheet. Bake for 12-15 minutes or until golden brown and just firm to the touch. Lay a teatowel on top, and invert a wire rack over the teatowel.

Turn the soufflé base over and cover with a second teatowel so it doesn't dry out.

Mix the cream into the mussels and spread them over the surface of the soufflé base. With the help of the teatowel, roll up the roulade. If to be served warm, the roulade should be wrapped in foil and gently heated in a 150°C / 300°F / Gas 2 oven for 10-15 minutes. If to be served cold, chill it to facilitate slicing.

MUSSEL CLAFOUTIS

A sort of mussel Toad in the Hole: you can make it with mussels alone, or in combination with other goodies such as mushrooms, bacon or fish chunks. Bake it in one dish or in individual ones. Serve for supper with a salad.

SERVES 3-4

250 g / 9 oz cleaned, cooked and	*pepper*
shelled mussels (pages 145-6),	*100 g / 3¹/₂ oz (US ²/₃ cup) flour*
with 125 ml / 4 fl oz of the	*4 eggs*
juice	*snipped chives*
125 ml / 4 fl oz milk	*oil*

Heat the oven to 220°C / 425°F / Gas 7.

Blend together in the blender or food processor the mussel juice, milk, pepper, flour, eggs and chives. Put a film of oil into a heavy ovenproof dish and heat it in the oven. Pour in the custard mixture and dot the mussels on top. Bake in the preheated oven for 25-30 minutes until golden and well risen.

MUSSELS AND FISH IN BRIK (OR PHYLLO) PARCELS WITH CREAMY RED PEPPER SAUCE

Chunks of fish and mussels are wrapped in a pastry parcel, briefly roasted and served over a creamy purée of red pepper.

SERVES 4

2 kg / 4½ lb mussels
500 g / 1 lb 2 oz firm fish fillets, skinless
4 brik leaves 20 cm / 8 inches in diameter, or 4 sheets phyllo pastry about 20 cm / 8 inches square

pepper
1 red sweet pepper: about 150 g / 5 oz
150 ml / 5 fl oz cream
olive oil

Clean, cook and shell the mussels as in the general instructions (pages 145-6). Strain the juice through a piece of muslin or cheesecloth or a nappy or diaper liner and reserve 150 ml / 5 fl oz.

Cut the fish fillet into cubes about the size of the mussels. Divide the fish cubes and mussels among the brik leaves (or phyllo sheets), piling them up in the middle.

Season with pepper only. Bring the sides up to make four-cornered parcels and place them seam sides down on a board.

Sear the red pepper over a gas flame or under the grill (US broiler) until thoroughly charred. Wrap in a teatowel and put in a plastic bag for 20 minutes. Then rub off the skin under running water, remove the stalk and seeds, and cut into chunks. Put in a pan with the mussel juice and the cream. Simmer gently for 5 minutes. Liquidize until quite smooth. Return to the pan to simmer 5 minutes more.

Shortly before serving, heat the oven to 200°C / 400°F / Gas 6. Brush the parcels with olive oil and place on a baking sheet. Bake for 5-6 minutes or until golden brown and a little crispy. The fish, visible through the pastry, should be just opaque.

Heat the sauce, pour it on to heated plates and place the parcels on top, seam side uppermost. Serve with mixed long-grain and wild rice.

ROCKET

RUCOLA SATIVA

F: Roquette. G: Salatrauke. Rocket (alias arugula, or rucola) is all the rage nowadays. The way some chefs talk about it, you might think they had invented it, or at least discovered it. Yet it seems to have been a favourite little medicinal and salad plant for hundreds of years. Galen, the second century Greek physician, certainly knew of it, for he forbade the eating of it in salads without either purslane or lettuce. Play-going Greeks (according to Lynda Brown in *The Cook's Garden*) nibbled on it as they enjoyed themselves at Aristophanes' latest comedy. The Romans, too, appeared to appreciate the peppery flavour of both leaves and seeds. After the Great Fire of London in 1666 it sprang up among the ruins so prolifically that it 'created astonishment and wonder'. Traditional folk medicine prescribed it as an end-of-winter cure for tiredness and debility; it was an ingredient in cough syrups and enjoyed a certain reputation as a remedy for both baldness and impotence. Gerard the herbalist made the curious claim that anyone who ate rocket seeds before being flogged would not feel any pain. History doesn't relate whether he tried it out himself.

Gradually over the years it seemed to fall from favour, disappearing from both herbals and cookery texts. Country people in areas where it grew wild have always appreciated it, particularly in times of hardship. In the département of the Var during the war years, it was extensively gathered (along with various other wild plants ranging from poppies to teazles, nettles and dandelions) to liven up what must otherwise have been a fairly monotonous diet.

Now suddenly, here is rocket back to stardom again. Along with oakleaf lettuce (red and green), cos or romaine lettuce, curly endive, broad-leaved escarole and other chicories, plus feathery plumes of chervil, it enters into the composition of the fashionable Provençal salad mixture known as *mesclun*, crates of which are daily flown out of Nice airport to top restaurants around the world. Californian cooks grow their own rocket and make free with it; Italian restaurants serve it in salads with only the best virgin olive oil and on pasta; even the British have heard of it. A fiery little plant native to Mediterranean and Middle Eastern areas, it has dark green, deeply lobed, highly spicy leaves, very similar to the leaves of a radish. In the warm climates where it thrives, it germinates, flowers, bolts and subsequently seeds itself in quick succession, assuring a more or less continuous crop throughout the year. It is no surprise to find that rocket is

150

related to those other spicy members of the crucifer family: mustard, cress and radish (its leaves very closely resemble radish leaves). Its seeds are used in some southern countries instead of mustard to make a particularly pungent relish. Rich in natural oils (30%) the seeds are pressed to give a beautiful pale golden oil. The characteristic pepperiness fades as the oil ages, and it is particularly valued by some for preserving vegetables. The leaves are a most welcome addition to winter salads, whether composed mainly of pulses or legumes (chick peas, haricots or other white beans, flageolets) or of sundry greenery.

If you live in a part of the world where rocket does not occur spontaneously, you can always cheat and buy the seeds. For a few francs in any French seed merchant's you can invest in a packet of rocket (or indeed *mesclun*, which comes ready mixed) and sow your own. If you sow it in late summer, by autumn it will be well underway and will go right on through the winter, apparently impervious to all but the fiercest frosts. With a bit of luck it may even run to seed. Then you can pretend that it got there all by itself.

ROCKET 'PESTO'

A wonderful green sauce which can be used for pasta, for potato salad or as a dip. The addition of cottage cheese lightens it considerably.

MAKES ABOUT 350 ML / 12 FL OZ

2 handfuls rocket leaves (US arugula), trimmed: about 75 g / 2½ oz
2 cloves garlic, crushed
optional: 50 g / scant 2 oz (US ½ cup) pine nuts
salt
200 g / 7 oz cottage cheese
6 tbsp olive oil
2 tbsp grated Parmesan

Put the rocket leaves in the food processor or blender with the garlic, pine nuts (if used), salt and cottage cheese. Blend or process until smooth. With the motor running, pour in the oil in a steady stream, stopping now and then to scrape down the sides. Finally add the Parmesan. Keep in a covered pot in the fridge until needed.

CHICORY, BLUE CHEESE AND ROCKET SPIRALS WITH SOFT-BOILED EGGS AND BACON

A decorative and delicious winter salad, which can be prepared ahead except for the last-minute bacon bits. To get the spiral effect, you must dismantle the chicons, spread the leaves with a tasty mixture and re-assemble for slicing over the salad.

SERVES 4

2 large heads of chicory (US Belgian endive)

100g / 3½oz blue cheese: Bleu d'Auvergne, Stilton or similar

2 tbsp fromage frais or Greek yogurt

25g / scant 1oz (US 1½ tbsp) soft butter

50g / scant 2oz cream cheese or cottage cheese

black pepper

2 small bunches rocket (US arugula) or salad burnet: about 50g / scant 2oz

100ml / 3½ floz oil

2 tbsp vinegar

a pinch each salt, pepper and dry mustard

1 tsp sugar

a splash Worcestershire sauce

1 tbsp plain yogurt

8 walnut halves, chopped

2 eggs

100g / 3½oz piece streaky bacon, rind removed, diced small

Cut a good slice off the root end of the chicory heads and lift away each of the leaves. Keep cutting a little off the ends as necessary to enable you to remove more leaves. Leave a hearty bit in the middle. Set the leaves aside.

In the food processor or blender, mix together to a smooth paste the blue cheese, *fromage frais* or yogurt, soft butter, cream or cottage cheese, black pepper to taste and half of the rocket. Spread the chicory leaves with a layer of this mixture, then press them back together again to reassemble the head. Wrap each one tightly in clingfilm (like a Christmas cracker) and refrigerate till firm (at least an hour).

Mix together the oil, vinegar, salt, pepper, mustard, sugar, Worcestershire sauce and yogurt to make a vinaigrette. Stir in the chopped walnuts. Cook the eggs in boiling water for 8 minutes, drain, refresh under cold running water and peel. Cut into eighths.

To serve, toss the remaining rocket or salad burnet leaves in the dressing and arrange them on 4 plates. Slice the reassembled, stuffed chicory about ½ cm / ¼ inch thick and arrange them over the salad leaves. Distribute the eggs decoratively around. Fry the bacon dice in a heavy pan without extra fat until golden and crusty. Sprinkle them over the salad. Spoon any extra dressing over and serve at once.

THREE-COLOURED BEAN SALAD

A lovely winter salad to go with cold meats.

SERVES 6

a 400g / 14oz can each of white haricot or cannellini, red kidney and green flageolet beans, drained
creamy dressing (page 6)

1 red or purple onion, finely chopped
2 handfuls rocket leaves (US arugula): about 50g / scant 2oz, shredded

Arrange the drained beans in their separate colours in an oblong or oval dish and add some dressing. Sprinkle on the onion and rocket leaves and chill well.

ROCKET, GARLIC CHEESE AND SWEETCORN GRATIN

Rocket leaves are blended or processed with garlic cheese, fromage frais, eggs and sweetcorn for a gratin which makes an excellent vegetarian dish or a good accompaniment for grilled or roasted white meats or cold ham. If you separate the yolks from the whites and beat the latter to a snow, you will get more of a soufflé effect.

SERVES 4

about 50g / scant 2oz rocket leaves (US arugula), finely chopped
150g / 5oz garlic cheese with herbs: Tartare, Boursin

150ml / 5floz fromage frais
salt and pepper
4 eggs
a 200g / 7oz can sweetcorn, drained

Butter an ovenproof gratin dish or soufflé dish, 1.1 litres / 2 pint (US 5 cup) capacity. Put the rocket leaves in the blender or food processor with the garlic cheese, fromage frais, salt, pepper and eggs. Blend or process roughly until mixed. Stir in the sweetcorn. Pour into the gratin dish.

Heat the oven to 180°C / 350°F / Gas 4. Bake for 30-40 minutes or until firm and golden. (The gratin cooks faster in a shallow gratin dish than in a deep soufflé dish.)

SLOE

PRUNUS SPINOSA

F: Prunelle (sauvage). G: Schwarzdorn, Schlehe. Prunus spinosa is a prickly beast. In order to brave the dangers of picking its bloomy fruit, it helps to understand the joys of sloe gin. Faithfully brewed in the pantries of English country houses since Victorian times, this wonderful drink (known in our family and probably others as 'sluggins') is a great way of converting a wholly unpalatable fruit into a rather memorable experience. A few other thrifty people have pursued an interest in these sour little plums. In the Black Forest as in Alsace a rare spirit is distilled from sloes, quite dry and different from sloe gin. In France the liqueur *prunelle* is flavoured with sloes, while a *confit* is made with sugar and spices, for serving with game or terrines.

Spring is the best time for sloe-spotting. Observe the edges of woods any time from March to May and the white flowers of the blackthorn are a giveaway. They are also a boon to bees, for whom they provide some of the earliest nectar sources. If you are superstitious, don't tempt fate by bringing blackthorn branches indoors: tradition has it that they bring bad luck, even a death. In Germany in the old days the branches played a part in the process of salt extraction. The bark, flowers and leaves are all used in folk medicine for various purposes. The wonderful hard wood of the blackthorn is used to make hammer shafts and handles for garden forks.

By late summer the berries begin to ripen, and by early autumn they are about the size of large peas (or small olives). As they ripen, their bluish black skin is covered with a delicious bloom. The flesh is mouth-puckeringly sour, but with a curious and distinctive flavour which comes through clearly in the liqueurs and spirits which are made from it. Having marked your tree in the spring, the time to go back to pick the fruit is after the first frost. By then, busy fingers or beaks may have beaten you to it so you can cheat by picking the sloes early and putting them in the deep freeze for a spell. Don a thick, spindle-proof coat for the expedition, and some good gloves. A brush with a blackthorn bush can be a very painful business.

A couple of good handfuls of these tiny plums is enough to make a bottle of sloe gin. The exercise may seem a bit of an extravagance, given the price of (British) gin nowadays, but it's eminently worth it. Doubtless things were different in Victorian times when sloes were free for the picking and gin dangerously cheap. Nowadays sloe gin comes into the category of a prized speciality, made by connoisseurs at home

SLOE GIN

Sloes, together with sugar and gin, make a warming winter liqueur, wonderful for cold shooting days or after a brisk walk in the country. I give you two recipes – one is my father's (via Constance Spry), the other from my friend Mrs Master. Try them both, and then have a (blind?) tasting.

DAD'S 'SLUGGINS'

MAKES ABOUT 1.5 LITRES/2¹⁄₃ PINTS (US 1¹⁄₂ QUARTS)

850g/1lb 14oz sloes
350g/12oz lump sugar, less if
* you like a sharper effect*

1¹⁄₂ bottles gin: 700ml size
a few drops almond essence (US
* almond extract)*

Remove the stalks and prick the sloes all over with a needle. Put them in a wide-necked bottle or jar with lid. Add the sugar, gin and almond essence. Leave to macerate for at least 4 months, turning the bottle gently and reverently from time to time to mix well. After this time (my father instructs succinctly), 'strain, and drink'.

(though Gordons make some around Christmas time, costing about £12 a bottle – about twice the price of the gin alone).

Though sloes can be added to other fruits to make jellies (see page 114 for apple, sloe and rosehip jelly) or to sharpen and confer their very special flavour to fruit purées, it is the liqueur which is their *raison d'être*. Save it for guests who really understand the compliment you are paying them, or use it sparingly to give a fillip to special sauces.

MRS MASTER'S SLOE GIN

In this recipe, the sloes are given a few days maceration with the sugar to encourage them to release some of their delicious juice.

MAKES ABOUT 1.25 LITRES/2 PINTS (US 5 CUPS)

500g/1lb 2oz sloes
100g/3¹/₂oz (US ¹/₂ cup) sugar
1 litre/1²/₃ pints (US 1 quart) gin
a few drops almond essence (US almond extract)

Remove the stalks and prick the sloes all over. Mix the fruit and sugar in a jar or crock, cover loosely and leave for 2-3 days, shaking and stirring daily until the juice begins to run. Add the gin and almond essence. Cover tightly and leave for 3 months in a dark place, shaking occasionally. Filter and bottle the liqueur and leave to mature for at least 6 months. (The 6-month period – and the quantity of resulting liqueur – tends to get whittled down due to the frequent samplings necessary.)

PORK TENDERLOIN IN A CREAMY SLOE GIN SAUCE

This recipe is quite extravagant on the sloe gin, but you won't regret it. If you have time, marinate the pork in it for a day or two beforehand, then drain and pat it dry before browning. Serve with ribbon noodles and broccoli.

SERVES 4

2 pork fillets/tenderloins: each about 300g/10oz
salt and pepper
25g/scant 1oz (US 1¹/₂ tbsp) butter
1 tsp oil
1 shallot, finely chopped
150ml/5floz sloe gin
300ml/10floz beef stock, or water + ¹/₂ beef stock cube
150ml/5floz double cream (US heavy cream) or crème fraîche

Season the tenderloins and brown them briskly in hot butter and oil on all sides in a heavy casserole (with a lid for later). Remove them. Lower the heat and in the same fat soften the shallot gently. Return the pork to the casserole, pour over the sloe gin and stock, cover and simmer gently for about 20 minutes or until just cooked – the meat should feel firm and springy to the touch. Do not overcook, or it will be dry. Remove the meat, wrap in foil and keep it warm. Reduce the cooking juices by half by fast boiling. Stir in the cream and reduce again by half. Check the seasoning.

The meat can either be carved at the table and the sauce served separately, or sliced and put into the sauce for a quick simmer before serving.

SLOWLY BRAISED BEEF WITH A SLOE FINISH

Sloe gin gives a delicious flavour and extra punch to a piece of beef gently braised with wine and spices. The sauce is made from a reduction of the cooking juices with a *schuss* of sloe gin at the end. Serve in thick slices with baked potatoes and crunchy cooked green cabbage.

SERVES 6

WITH SECOND HELPINGS

a 1.6 kg / 3½ lb piece of braising beef, tied in a neat bolster
salt and pepper
optional: some split beef or calf bones
2 tbsp oil, or 25 g / scant 1 oz duck or goose fat
4 tbsp sloe gin
2 carrots, sliced
1 large onion, sliced
1 clove garlic, peeled
1 stalk celery or a piece celeriac (US celery root)

½ bottle cheap but drinkable red wine: Beaujolais Primeur works well
about 300 ml / 10 fl oz beef stock, or water + ½ a beef stock cube
a bayleaf
a sprig sage
1 tsp cornflour (US cornstarch) or arrowroot, if needed

Season the meat and brown it all over (along with the bones, if used) in the hot fat. Spoon over 2 tbsp of sloe gin and let it cook for a few minutes more. Remove the meat (and bones). Lower the heat and in the same fat (add a little more if necessary to film the bottom of the pan), cook the carrots, onion, garlic and celery or celeriac gently for about 10 minutes. Replace the meat (and bones), pour on the wine and add enough stock to come about two-thirds of the way up the meat. Add the herbs. Cover with foil and a lid. Either cook gently on top of the stove or in a 150°C / 300°F / Gas 2 oven for 2-2½ hours. Check occasionally: the liquid should be barely murmuring.

When the cooking time is up, remove the meat (which will have shrunk alarmingly) from the cooking juices. Discard the herbs. Mash the vegetables into the cooking liquid (or liquidize). Bring to a boil and check the seasoning. If the thickness is to your liking, simply stir in the remaining 2 tbsp sloe gin. Otherwise, mix the cornflour or arrowroot in the sloe gin and add to the liquid. Simmer for 10 minutes more, stirring occasionally, until correctly thickened. (The meat and sauce can be prepared ahead up to this point, and refrigerated.)

When ready to serve, remove the strings from the meat, slice it rather thickly and put it back in the casserole. Heat the sauce and pour it over and around the meat. Reheat gently on top of the stove or in a low oven for 20-30 minutes.

Duperrex, Aloys, Poluzzi, Charles and Dougoud, Roger, *Unsere Pilze*, Avanti Club, Neuchâtel

Fernie, W. T., *Meals Medicinal with Herbal Simples (of Edible Parts)*, John Wright & Co, Bristol 1905

Gardet, Claude, *Les secrets des herbes de Provence*, Secalib, 1984

Gibbons, Euell, *Stalking the Wild Asparagus*, David McKay Co. Inc., New York 1962

Grigson, Jane, *Fruit Book*, Penguin London 1983
 – *The Mushroom Feast*, Penguin, London 1975

Koechlin-Schwartz, Dorothée & Grapas, Martine, *Guide de l'anti-consommateur*, Ed. Seghers, Paris 1975

Kybal, Jan, *Plantes aromatiques et culinaires* (trad. Barbara Faure), ARTIA, Prague 1981

Lánská, Dabmar, *Plantes sauvages et comestibles*, (trad. Dagmar Doppia), Aventinum, Prague 1992

Lang, George, *The Cuisine of Hungary*, Penguin, London 1985

Loewenfeld, Clare, *Britain's Wild Larder: Fungi*, Faber & Faber, London 1956

Luard, Elisabeth, *European Festival Food*, Bantam Press, London 1990

Mabey, Richard, *Food for Free*, Collins, London 1972
 – *Plants with a purpose*, Collins, London 1977

Mazille, La, *La bonne cuisine du Périgord*, Flammarion, Paris 1929

Moreau, Claude, *Guide des champignons comestibles et vénéneux*, Larousse, Paris 1988

Phillips, Roger, *Wild Food*, Pan Books, London 1983
 – *Mushrooms*, Pan Books, London 1981

Richardson, Rosamond, *Hedgerow Cookery*, Penguin, London 1980

Rothmayr, Julius, *Essbare und giftige Pilze des Waldes*, E. Haag, Luzern 1916

Schretzenmayr, Martin, *Heimische Bäume und Sträucher Mitteleuropas*, Ferdinand Enke Verlag, Stuttgart 1990

Sélection du Reader's Digest, *Secrets et vertus des plantes médicinales*, Paris 1985

Strang, Jeanne, *Goose Fat and Garlic*, Kyle Cathie, London 1991

Wagner, C., *Die Pilz-Küche*, W. Hepting, Andelfingen 1943

White, Florence, *Flowers as Food*, Jonathan Cape, London 1934